THE POWER OF GOD'S HEALING LOVE

MARRIAGE ON THE MEND

JOYCE HUGGETT

INTERVARSITY PRESS
DOWNERS GROVE, ILLINOIS 60515

© 1988 by Joyce Huggett

Published in the United States of America by InterVarsity Press, Downers Grove, Illinois, with permission
from Kingsway Publications Ltd., Eastbourne, E. Sussex, England.

InterVarsity Press is the book-publishing division of InterVarsity Christian Fellowship, a student movement
active on campus at hundreds of universities, colleges and schools of nursing. For information about local
and regional activities, write Public Relations Dept., InterVarsity Christian Fellowship, 6400 Schroeder Rd.,
P.O. Box 7895, Madison, WI 53707-7895.

Distributed in Canada through InterVarsity Press, 860 Denison St., Unit 3, Markham, Ontario L3R 4H1,
Canada.

All Scripture quotations, unless otherwise indicated, are from the Holy Bible, New International Version.
Copyright © 1973, 1978, International Bible Society. Used by permission of Zondervan Bible Publishers.

Cover photograph: Carlos Vergara

ISBN 0-8308-1255-5

Printed in the United States of America

Library of Congress Cataloging-in-Publication Data

Huggett, Joyce, 1937-
   Marriage on the mend.

   Bibliography: p.
    1. Marriage—Religious aspects—Christianity.
2. Huggett, Joyce, 1937-   . I. Title.
BV835.H82 1988   248.4   88-6840
ISBN 0-8308-1255-5

16	15	24	13	12	11	10	9	8	7	6	5	4	3	2	1
99	98	97	96	95	94	93	92	91	90	89	88				

For Derek and Maureen
with love and thanks for years
of friendship and supportive prayer.

———————————

Thanks also to John Sayers for the use of his poem on
pages 85-86, Frank Booth for allowing me to
reproduce his diagrams and the couples who have
given ready permission for their
stories to be told in this book.

Preface

Stories of broken marriages have been hitting the headlines in the national press for years now. As I write I have in front of me several newspaper clippings reminding me of that fact. One is page three of the London *Daily Mail*, published on Saturday, May 12, 1984. An eye-catching photograph of an attractive thirty-three-year-old woman with her five children sits alongside the huge headline: *Lock the Doors So Daddy Won't Leave Again.*

The story centers around a soccer personality who had left his wife and children for a younger woman but who was now "under heavy and heart-tugging pressure from his five children to return and stay with them for good." The article records the wife's hopes that their marriage could be mended:

"Last time he came home he said he still had a deep affection for me. He is a family man and I think that in the end his conscience will bring him back to me. The children's joy at having their father back—even temporarily—is overwhelming. The last time the family were together, five-year-old Emily tied [her father's] shoe laces together and told him, 'Now you have to stay here for ever and ever.' "

To her mother the little girl said, "Why don't you lock all the doors so Daddy won't leave again?"

And the youngest child, aged three, asked, "Why has another lady taken Daddy away?"

A story published in the *London Times* a month earlier, April 18, 1984, carries this headline: *When a Vicar Leaves Home.* This story describes how, after seventeen years of marriage, a certain pastor left his wife and their three children. The story records the feelings of "anguish and isolation" experienced by the wife who suddenly found herself homeless.

Splashed across yet another newspaper, this headline catches the reader's eye: *Vicar Returns after Death of His Wife.* This time the reporter tells how a pastor's wife was found dead with pills at her bedside after she had discovered that her husband was having an affair with another woman.

I have in front of me also several Christian magazines which highlight the seriousness of the situation in the West today. I quote from just one of them: "Breakdown in marriage is running at around 150,000 divorces a year . . . one for every three marriages. Those marriages most at risk are those who marry under the age of 21; those who have known one another little before marriage; and those cases in which the bride is already pregnant."[1]

Marital breakdown, it seems, is news; of interest to everyone.

But I have in front of me also a pile of letters, books and tapes which suggest to me that, as Christians, we have news of a rather different kind to spread abroad. It is sensational news. News which should surely hit the headlines of every national newspaper and every Christian publication. News which, sadly, scarcely receives a mention anywhere. It is this: At a time when government statistics show that between one in two and one in three marriages are breaking down, many, many broken marriages are being mended. The couples concerned are enjoying an unprecedented degree of intimacy in the very relationship which they once considered dead. This curious state of affairs must surely be a modern miracle.

I first bumped into this miracle in 1969 when I read a book called *Death and Rebirth of a Marriage* (Scripture Union) in which the authors, Alan and Margaret Havard, bravely testified to the goodness of God in restoring their relationship after it had deteriorated seriously. I next experienced this miracle in the 1970s when the finger of God touched my own marriage and gave my husband and me the joy of discovering what Christian marriage was really all about. After that, I met miracle after miracle in such quick succession that I made the observation to a friend, "This is good news! It ought to be broadcast."

For the past year, that casual remark dropped in a friend's listening ear has grown in my mind like a sapling gradually gaining strength. The conviction that this news needs to be spread has also grown. And so this book was conceived. During the gestation period of the past twelve months, I have observed closely some of the ways God is demonstrating the age-old truth that with him nothing is impossible; that he can even mend marriages which seem irreparable. I have watched with awe while he mended certain relationships known to me. Now the time has come to give birth to the book which bears this good news. I do so making no apologies for producing yet another book on marriage. Rather, I write this breathing a prayer that in some way this book may pierce the pessimism which seems to surround the marriage relationship today. I pray it can bring hope to those whose marriages are under pressure.

In order to be single minded in the writing of this book, I retreated to a small cottage in the country where I could pray and think and write to my heart's content. When I reached this cottage, the temperature had dropped to an all-time low, snow had fallen and, since someone had left the kitchen faucets dripping, the drain had frozen solid and water was trickling onto the newly carpeted kitchen floor. Before I could write a word, therefore, I was faced with the task of drying out the carpet and thawing the ice in the drain.

"Wrap a piece of cloth round the pipe and pour boiling water over it every twenty minutes or so," my husband advised when I called him for advice. I complied, and to my great delight, three hours later the offending block of ice finally fell from the pipe and I watched water freely flow down the drain.

As I settled to my work, I realized that this episode illustrated the central idea of marriage mending. What the newspapers and magazines focus on are frozen relationships, ice-bound marriages. But what my husband and I, together with many others, see God doing over and over again is melting the blockages so that the couples concerned can enjoy not simply the thawing of their relationships but the springtime which always follows the chill of winter. It is my prayer that through this book God will free up blocked relationships and that couples whose marriages seemed locked in eternal winter may yet discover the spring-time of their marriage which is just around the corner. This indeed can happen as they find afresh the love which returns to those who seek to love each other within the love of God.

CHAPTER 1

WITH GOD NOTHING IS IMPOSSIBLE

G OD GOES ABOUT MENDING BROKEN THINGS." THAT SLOGAN once appeared on a poster by Oxfam, a self-help development agency. I borrowed the saying for the title of my first book's final chapter. The book was called *Two into One*—a marriage book primarily for newlyweds. In that final chapter I made this statement:

That poster claims that God goes about mending broken things. . . . This God is a creative God. It was he who brooded over darkness and emptiness and created light, life, beauty and delicacy. His activity is also re-creative. He is the potter whose skilled and sensitive

hands reshape persons, nations and relationships. . . . God does go
about mending things, including splintered marriages.[2]
I believed that bold claim. Even so, when Sally told me her story just
before my book was published, I was bowled over by the mystery and
generosity of the God who still goes around mending broken marriages.

I first met Sally one February night, at midnight. We had both been
attending a writers' workshop, and although I had felt drawn to this
attractive, vivacious, gregarious American the moment she spoke up in
the seminars we had both attended, the timetable had been so full that
we had had no chance to talk until now—the last night of the conference when most people were saying their good-bys.

We happened to be standing next to one another in a group of
people who were chattering happily, and I was determined not to lose
this chance to tell her how much I had appreciated her comments in
the seminars. I had not expected, when I started that conversation, that
Sally would underline for me a claim which I had so recently penned
and which was shortly to be published: namely, that God comes into
our darkness as light, that he broods over the chaos of our disintegrating relationships and reshapes them, that he re-creates them so that
they are as new.

Sally and Richard's Story

Sally and her English husband, Richard, had been married for seven
years when their splintering marriage finally broke. Neither of them
were Christians at the time and neither of them knew of anyone in
whom to confide until American friends of Sally's descended on them
quite out of the blue. When Sally confided in them that Richard was
having an affair with another woman and that her marriage seemed to
be in ruins, these friends suggested that she should return to the States
with them for a while. This she did, and while she was taking refuge

in their home they talked to her about God, the Friend they had met for themselves only recently. They suggested to Sally that, just as God had helped them through various crises, so he could help her. They went further and suggested that Sally might ask this God to help her. To her own amazement, Sally found herself praying one day. And to her even greater amazement, she discovered that, when she prayed, some of the heaviness which had been weighing on her lifted; she became aware of an overwhelming sense of power which she took to be the power of God. Since God was meeting her in such an effective way, she decided to hand over her life to him, to enlist as a member of Christ's kingdom.

Happy in her new faith and supported by her recently converted friends, Sally decided to settle in the U.S. She applied for a job, was offered it and was just about to accept it when the realization dawned that God was asking her to return to England to her husband. But when she returned to England, Richard did not welcome her with open arms. He was still infatuated with the other woman, and Sally's arrival was an unwelcome intrusion.

Nevertheless, for two more years Sally and Richard lived under the same roof. These proved to be two years of growing animosity and pain. Although Richard could see that a huge transformation had taken place in his wife, that her aggressiveness and moodiness had been re-placed with gentleness and an even-temperedness, he decided that a future with Sally was unthinkable. Their years together had inflicted too many wounds for them to take the risk of beginning life together again. They decided to divorce.

The proceedings dragged on, month in, month out. Richard's rela-tionship with the other woman became increasingly strained, and Rich-ard despaired. One day, he telephoned the Samaritans, a nationwide network of caring volunteers, and asked to speak to a Christian counselor. A Christian counselor was found eventually, and his acceptance of Richard as a person and his genuine concern for the situation made a deep impression on Richard. When this counselor suggested that Richard should invite God into the turmoil, Richard took the advice seriously. After the counselor had left him, Richard prayed that God would take over the steering-wheel of his life. Relief and wonder overwhelmed him, the burdens of years seemed to leave him and he tasted for himself the refreshment and healing God's love brings.

Although both Richard and Sally were now Christians, their relationship had been so full of bitterness and backbiting that neither of them knew how to pick up the pieces of their shattered marriage. They agreed that the best policy would be to allow divorce proceedings to continue.

Two months after Richard turned to Christ, he and Sally were invited to a friend's party. It was Christmas morning. When the party was over and the guests were departing, the alienated husband and wife were alone for a few moments, just looking at one another across the room. They had not looked at one another in this way for years. Suddenly, Richard's heart filled with regret as memories of the wasted years rose before him like a specter. Could they possibly begin again?

The room was empty now. He walked across that room to the place where Sally was sitting and offered her his hand to help her up. As he did so, the ice in his heart began to melt. He and Sally clung to each other, tears pouring down their faces. It was as though the block stopping the flow of love had been dislodged, and the love which had eluded them for years came flooding back into both of them. They walked away from that Christmas-morning party man and wife in the truest sense of that phrase. They were one—united in love.

A few days later, a letter arrived informing them of the date of the divorce hearing. They tore it up. The God who had touched first Sally as an individual and then Richard as an individual was now touching the Richard-Sally unit—their relationship.

He was giving them a brand new start in marriage. The divorce hearing would not, therefore, be necessary.

After Sally had finished her story, I went home. Sleep eluded me for most of that night. I lay in bed with a glow of happiness warming me deep inside. At the same time my mind was working overtime as it tried to fathom what happens when God finds first one partner and then the other—and then gives them back to one another. What is the hidden, life-changing ingredient which makes such a miracle not only possible but common?

The Activating Agent

I thought of salt and then meditated on the fact that it works on food in an unseen-but-beneficial way. I also thought of yeast and its hidden-but-effective work which causes a lump of dough to rise. And I realized that when a person turns to Christ, an activating agent like this must be powerfully at work.

Some words of Paul flashed across the screen of my mind as though to confirm my thoughts: "God has poured out his love into our hearts by the Holy Spirit, whom he has given us" (Rom 5:5). Of course! The Christian is being acted upon by a hidden agent who is far more effective and powerful than yeast or salt. This active ingredient is none other than the Holy Spirit of God himself. It is the same Spirit who raised Jesus from the dead. No wonder a miracle happened to Richard and Sally's marriage when both of them capitulated to the Spirit of God. Rather than being surprised when such wonderful things happen, maybe we should even be expecting a tidal wave of such marriage-mending miracles. When God intervenes, the God with whom nothing is impossible, a supernatural power is unleashed and the impossible becomes possible.

I was soon to learn what I had not appreciated before—that God is working this miracle regularly. In one sense, the way he does it is unique to each relationship needing repair. In another sense, the couples concerned all experience something similar happening to them. The heavenly potter seems to look down on the fragments of a marriage which began with high hopes and expectations but which has since been shattered. With skillful hands he gathers up the scattered pieces, melts them, molds them and then reshapes them, making of them a vessel far more beautiful than the original—and far more useful. He then fills the re-created vessel with his life-giving Spirit so that the couple may pour out to others the comfort and help with which they were once supported.

This has certainly happened for Richard and Sally. I stayed in their home recently and observed for myself the lovely relationship which God has given them. And when I spoke to Sally to ask her permission to use their story in this book, she agreed readily and added, "Tell them it's getting better and better all the time."

But theirs is not a selfish love. Because God moved into an impossible situation and mended their marriage in such a miraculous way, their hearts go out to couples whose marriages are under stress. God has gifted them with the ability to become instruments of his healing to such people.[3]

Bob and Pat's Story

Unlike Richard and Sally, Bob and Pat's relationship had not been killed by bitter arguments and infidelity. Rather, during their twenty-year marriage, the dry rot of boredom and overfamiliarity had set in. As Bob explained to me, "Sadly, when you've been married for twenty years you can just drift apart, take each other for granted and basically not communicate. You know how your partner will respond to any given circumstance, so you don't bother to enquire and chat anymore. That was the point we'd reached."

As Bob told me how God stepped in and arrested the malaise, I was conscious again that the mysterious hidden ingredient, the Holy Spirit of Jesus, had been active in this relationship, too, quietly and gradually transforming it.

Bob, a farmer, was a regular churchgoer. He was a church lay leader and treasurer, working hard for his village and his pastor. However, after twenty years of working for God, he discovered that he did not know the God he heard about in church Sunday after Sunday. God longs to be found, and when a man begins the search he goes more than half way to meet him. God brought alongside Bob a friend who had recently come into a living faith. She invited Bob and Pat to her church when Michael Green was preaching. In the course of the sermon Michael Green explained how a person can find God. Prayer, he said, was the key: "If you want to find God, just get on your knees and pray." Bob had been sitting on the edge of his seat throughout the sermon. So much of it seemed addressed just to him. So when Michael Green invited people to pray, Bob prayed. Nothing happened. Two days later still nothing had happened. Bob felt distraught and cheated. It was as though he had been led to the threshold of heaven only to find the gates barred against him.

On the third morning, however, all this changed. Bob remembers:

I woke up a completely transformed character. I had new eyes to see with, new ears and a new appreciation of the world and the people in it. Somehow I knew that God had answered my prayer; I knew Jesus was my Savior. One of the first things he did for me was to cause me to fall in love with my wife all over again. I said I had new eyes and new ears. I began to see my own wife with whom I'd lived for twenty years in a new way and I began to appreciate her again. Pat, too, came to know the Lord in a meaningful way and from that point on the Lord transformed our relationship.

I worked with Bob and Pat recently and observed for myself the way God uses them to come alongside others with supportive, caring love. And I made a mental note of the fact that what God has done in them and for them he is now doing through them. He delights to use "wounded healers."

Though friends like Richard and Sally, and Bob and Pat, shared their story with me, it was not until the spring of 1985 that I fully realized the extent to which God is moving around Britain performing the kind of miracle I have described. But in February and March of that year I bumped into so many couples who had been on the receiving end of this marriage-mending miracle that I was forced to take notice.

I was touring England with four other speakers, visiting the centers where Billy Graham had preached the previous summer. An enterprising woman in Birmingham had organized a day conference for women in each of these centers and I conducted a seminar called "A New Recipe for Marriage."

Overwhelmed and intrigued by the response to these rallies, we set ourselves the task of discovering why hundreds of women had made the effort to attend. I began each seminar by asking a question: "Why, when you had a choice of five seminars, did you select this one on marriage?" Although several hundred women were present on each occasion, embarrassment did not prevent several of them from spreading their good news.

On one occasion, a woman testified that she and her husband had been married for thirty-two years. After twenty-eight years, they separated. Both had since come to faith in Christ during meetings at which Billy Graham was speaking. This newfound love for God enabled them to rediscover their love for one another. Once again, they were living as husband and wife, reconciled with one another through God. "This time we want ours to be a Christian marriage," the woman admitted. "That's why I've come to your seminar."

On the same day, another woman explained what had pushed her into coming to a seminar to study God's recipe for marriage. She told us that she had been married for twenty-five years. She had turned to Christ many years earlier and had since prayed regularly for her husband. "God has just given me a wonderful silver-wedding present," she said. "My husband has just become a believer. Our relationship has changed already. But we want to learn what a Christian marriage really means. That's why I've come to your seminar."

Just as dew falling on fields saturates them, so the Holy Spirit of God is falling on the hard hearts of people, softening them, preparing them to be melted back into a oneness with their partners in marriage. But God is doing this not just for couples newly converted to Christianity. He is also doing it for couples whose belief is strong, whose experience of God's love is long but whose marriages have fallen into a state of disrepair. One of the most moving examples of this is the miracle God worked for David and Gwen Wilkerson.

Gwen's Testimony

In her book *In His Strength*, Gwen Wilkerson traces the history of her husband's ministry—first as an evangelist, then as a pastor and finally as a youth worker. She describes how he became involved with Teen Challenge, the organization which aims to reach for Christ the gangs and drug addicts thronging the streets of New York City. And, with moving frankness, she reveals the cost this ministry exacted on their marriage.

While her husband fast became a celebrity, partly through a ministry

which won thousands for Christ and partly through his writing, she
stayed at home rearing their children. She shares how she sought to be
mother and father to the children in their father's absence, how she
battled with cancer as well as her growing feelings of jealousy and anger.
While her husband's fame increased, she and the children were being
neglected.

"What about us?" I'd ask myself and the Lord. "What about his
own children? What about me? Don't we matter at all? Why isn't
he here taking care of his church and family?"[4]

Finally thoughts of separation and divorce not only entered Gwen's
mind but became almost attractive. "If my husband was going to spend
the rest of his life taking care of everyone's problems but mine, it
seemed that a life apart from him was the only answer for me."[5]

Thoughts like these dominated Gwen's thinking as she and her husband flew to California for a "second honeymoon." Almost as soon
as they checked into their hotel, while Dave was supposed to be preparing to speak at a banquet that very evening, they started shouting
insults at one another. Dave stalked out of the room, slamming the
door, and Gwen was left alone. Her husband did not return that day.
But fifteen minutes before the banquet was due to begin, he sent an
escort to accompany his wife to the banqueting hall. Gwen was furious.
But let her take up the story for herself:

David was to be the keynote speaker at the dinner and after that was
to address a city-wide rally at the civic auditorium. When my escort
and I arrived at the banquet hall, my husband was already seated at
the head table, looking for all the world like a man without a single
troubled thought. His apparent lack of concern added fuel to my
anger. Nevertheless, I made myself smile sweetly at the people to
whom I was being introduced as I was seated at a side-table. "He's
a big hypocrite, that's what he is!" I wanted to tell them all. "He'll

get up there and talk about God and everyone will think he's wonderful. No one will know that he doesn't even care about his wife any more. . . ."

Right after the meal was served, Dave slipped out, as he always did before he was to speak. I knew that he had gone off by himself to pray. "He'd better pray," I thought. "He's going to need a lot of help from God to pull this one off."

Although I didn't note what time David left, I became increasingly aware that he was gone longer than usual. The master of ceremonies was beginning to look a bit uneasy before he finally reappeared to take the podium. "Probably found out that God doesn't listen to hypocrites," I speculated, as he began to talk. Dave appeared to be speaking with no difficulty, however.

When the banquet was over, Dave and Gwen were whisked off to a large auditorium where five thousand people had gathered to hear a talk on the power and love of God—given by a man whose wife had decided to divorce him for neglect. Here's what Gwen saw:

Many of the faces around me were young faces—teenagers who were looking for answers to the problems life poses. They believed that David Wilkerson had some of the answers, and their faces were aglow with expectation and openness. Just looking at them brought me close to tears. How could David introduce them to the One who holds the key, when he was unable to find His help for us? Suddenly I was sure it had been a mistake for me to come hear him speak tonight, but the program was already beginning and it was too late for me to escape.

What followed remains wonderfully inexplicable. David's talk was aimed at the young people and was a simple message about the love of Jesus. I'd heard him present similar talks before. There was nothing unusual about the words he was saying or about his manner

of delivering them. Although I was only half-listening, I watched
him with what appeared to be rapt attention. Suddenly I became
aware that an aura of light surrounded him. I knew I was seeing a
work of the Lord—an anointing of His Holy Spirit on this man who
I was reviling in my thoughts.

"How can it be," I wondered, "that the Lord would use him when
everything is so wrong in his private life? How can He fill anyone
so unworthy with His own precious Spirit?"

Then the Lord Himself gave me the answer to my questions. The
glow that surrounded David began to fall also on me and I became
aware of the awesome presence of Jesus with me. From head to toe
I was immersed in a delicious warmth until all of a sudden I felt
completely at one with God.

I knew that a healing was taking place, though I could not guess
the profound nature of that healing. I only knew that when I looked
back at David he was looking straight at me, and that special spark
of recognition was lit between us once again. The Spirit was clearly
working on both of us simultaneously. Tears began to find their way
down my cheeks and fell unchecked onto my dress as I began for
the first time in many months to praise God for His goodness and
mercy.

Moments later, Dave ended his talk almost abruptly. Forgetting
about everyone around me and unmindful of any unseemliness in
my behavior, I ran backstage to find my husband. He was running
toward the auditorium to look for me, and we met in a crushing
embrace. Laughing and crying at the same time, we carried on like
a couple of kids in love who hadn't seen each other for months—
and really, I guess, we hadn't.[6]

That night David said his customary good-bys earlier than usual. Then,
arm in arm, he and Gwen hurried back to their hotel. They were still

grinning at each other. They extended their stay and enjoyed their "second honeymoon" after all. Gwen recalls:
It was worth waiting for. At first we just rejoiced in the healing of our marriage without trying to analyze what had happened. We knew that Jesus had done for us what we had been unable to do for ourselves—unlock the door to the love we had for each other, the love which He gave us in the beginning and which had never really died.[7]

The good news is that the God who poured this healing into Dave and Gwen Wilkerson's marriage continues to go around mending marriages—and his methods have not changed. Very often the healing takes place through a dramatic, divine intervention which is outside the control, though not outside the will, of the couple concerned. He delights to mend marriages which seemed beyond repair. He, who makes all things new, makes marriages new.

Sometimes the only method he seems to use is the kind of dynamic, supernatural intervention which defies analysis. More often, though, if my observation is correct, he brings about deep and lasting reconciliation between partners in marriage in another way. He touches the eyes of a couple's understanding, helps them to perceive what the essential ingredients of Christian marriages are, challenges them to take these ingredients on board, to work them into their own relationship. Then he anoints them with his Spirit while they work at this gargantuan task, showing them, in retrospect, that living biblically brings its own healing. This is how I sense God working over and over again.

And he starts by helping us "forsake all others"—persons and commitments—that might threaten the sanctity of the marriage.

CHAPTER 2

A NEW
NUMBER ONE

―――――――――

JESUS REFUSED TO REMAIN TIED TO HIS MOTHER'S APRON strings. As soon as he reached the age of maturity, he made it clear to Mary that he had one goal in life from which he would not waver: to discern the will of God in all things and to obey that perfect will implicitly. Whenever Mary seemed to suggest that he should sidestep from God's chosen path or interfere with God's timing, Jesus firmly rebuked her. So when she chastised him in the temple, he retorted, "Why were you searching for me? . . . Didn't you know I had to be in my Father's house?" (Lk 2:49).

At the wedding in Cana of Galilee he stalled her when she hinted that an immediate miracle might rescue their host and hostess from the embarrassment of running out of wine at the feast: "Dear woman. . . . My time has not yet come" (Jn 2:4). And later in his ministry, when his mother attempted to interrupt his work for God, Jesus reminded himself and the crowds that his life's work was to seek and to save those who would similarly obey his heavenly Father's voice (Mt 12:46-50). Nothing and no one would short-circuit this plan.

Yet Jesus' concern and expressed love for his mother knew no limits. We see this truth supremely illustrated at Calvary. While he hung on the cross, dying a criminal's death, his heart went out to his watching mother. Laying aside his own anguish and need, he recognized her need for support and companionship as she faced the sting of bereavement; he met this need by giving her his closest friend, John. It was John who recorded how, with great tenderness, Jesus demonstrated to Mary that he understood the bitter pain which filled her heart and mind and showed her that he wanted to alleviate her loneliness by offering her someone who would stand by her in her darkest hour. And so, looking at John, he whispered, "Dear woman, here is your son" (Jn 19:26). And to John he whispered, "Here is your mother" (Jn 19:27).

Jesus' Example

Jesus' example gives us two guidelines for adulthood which we must hold in tension. If we are truly to be free to hear the voice of God and obey it, we must, on the one hand, sever ourselves or be severed from any inappropriate tie that binds us to our parents and, at the same time, we must honor our parents and show them that we love them. We do this most effectively by recognizing what their needs really are and by being prepared, so far as we are able, to meet those needs lovingly, generously and at cost to ourselves. This applies to every adult whose desire it is to be transformed into the likeness of Christ. And in particular it applies to every Christian couple who is seeking to enjoy the quality of marital oneness God intends them to enjoy.

Recognition of the need to live biblically is a key factor in the mending of modern marriages. The first command God gives married couples is to move out of their parents' immediate orbit. This command, originally given at the beginning of time, pertains to every race and every generation: "Therefore a man leaves his father and his mother . . ." (Gen 2:24 RSV).

This command is repeated four times. In addition to its inclusion in Genesis 2, among God's first instructions to married people, we find it again in Matthew 19:5 and Mark 10:7, where Jesus assumes that his audience will have grasped the fact that this severance is foundational to healthy marriages. It is reiterated by Paul in Ephesians 5:31 where the apostle gives careful and detailed instructions to husbands and wives whose mission in life, he claims, is to create the kind of marriage which will reflect to the watching world the love which exists between Christ and his bride, the church. Its repetition, surely, has one chief purpose: that couples might sit up, take notice and act accordingly.

Miracles Happen

To *leave* means, among other things, that from the wedding day onward, the parents of the spouses must no longer take first place in their children's affection, thinking or planning, because from that day on the newlyweds both have a new number one: each other.

As I explained in my book *Two into One*, most couples who marry in an Anglican church dramatize this act of leaving during the marriage ceremony. The bride is brought to the church by her father who, in a ceremonial act, "gives her away" to the pastor, God's representative, who then gives her to her husband. This "giving away" is the first hint that a transaction is taking place, that the couple are on the threshold of making a brand-new relationship which is separate from both sets of parents.

Next, surrounded by parents and friends, best man and bridesmaids, relatives and other interested persons, the bride and groom make extensive promises: to love one another "for better, for worse, for richer, for poorer, in sickness and in health" and until death parts them. Having exchanged these and other solemn vows publicly for all to hear, and having exchanged rings, the pastor addresses the assembled congregation with the solemn words:

> In the presence of God, and before this congregation, N and N have given their consent and made their marriage vows to each other. They have declared their marriage by the joining of hands and by the giving and receiving of a ring. I therefore proclaim that they are husband and wife.

He goes on to exhort,

> That which God has joined together, let not man divide.[8]

In other words, no one and nothing must separate this couple who have become one in the sight and presence of God.

What happens next is significant. After the prayers, the sermon and the singing of a hymn or a psalm, the newlyweds walk away from their parents, the bridesmaids, the best man, the relatives and friends and, leaving all of these behind, move to the far end of the church where their marriage is lifted to God in prayer by the presiding pastor. This means that in visual terms the severance which is part of the act of leaving has now taken place; there is a space between the newlyweds and others which no one may violate.

What must now follow is that in their everyday lives the couple must be allowed similarly to walk away from everyone and everything so that a holy space is created around their relationship into which no one and nothing may stray. For it is within this vital space that the relationship is pushed along a notch. It is here that a deep, effective and lasting spiritual and emotional bonding is given the opportunity to germinate, grow and flourish between these two who seek both to retain their individuality and yet to become one.

When we think of weddings, we think of all the glorious paraphernalia: the bride's gown, the scent of the bouquets, the pomp and circumstance of the ceremony, the triumphant tone of the organ, the happy faces, the sense of anticipation, the generosity of well-wishers. This is the joyful face of leaving.

But leaving also has a painful face. I have already used the word *severance* to explain its meaning. *Severing, cutting, separating*: these are pain-filled words. As Walter Trobisch once reminded us, the leaving which is integral to healthy marriages is rather like the cutting of the umbilical cord when a baby is born. The midwife cuts that cord because the mother's role in the life of her child has changed. She is no longer required to feed her child intravenously. Now both she and the child must adapt to an entirely new method of relating. This new relationship possesses all the potential for intimacy, but it is different. And unless these differences are recognized and the cord is cut, the child will die.

What then happens is that the mother and baby discover the richness of this new relationship, and the bonding which takes place between them is a delight to watch and even more of a delight to participate in. But what is happening here is that a second umbilical cord is being formed. It is an invisible one since it is emotional this time and not physical. But, like the original cord, it ties the mother to the child. What Jesus' example shows us, and what must happen when a person marries, is that this cord too must be cut, not because the mother is redundant but because her role has changed yet again. She has fulfilled her task of nurturing her child emotionally and spiritually during the child's formative years. She must now let that child go. She must be prepared to make the adjustments which phase three of their relationship demands.

In this phase they may enjoy yet another dimension of intimacy, but her child must be given autonomy—set at liberty to try life his or her way, make mistakes without recrimination and form intimate attachments without reference to the parent figure. Unless this second umbilical cord is cut, the grown-up child's marriage may well die. And this is where parents feel the rub. (I write as a mother of adult children who feels keenly the sting of this severance.) And this is also where the mother-in-law problem ceases to be a comedy routine and becomes instead a thorn in the flesh of many a couple who try to live life God's way.

The thrilling thing is that where marriages have been marred by the interfering mother, God can step in and deal with the root of the problem—the uncut, invisible umbilical cord—and sever that cord so sensitively yet so effectively that these marriages are mended. Let me explain what I mean.

Doreen and Gordon's Story

Doreen was in considerable distress when she came to see me. She told me a story which was all too familiar, that her marriage was under stress and neither she nor her husband, Gordon, knew how to handle the situation.

Doreen and her mother had always enjoyed a close relationship, and she adored her father, who sacrificed himself endlessly for her. The problem was that when she married Gordon, she missed both the daddy-love her father had lavished on her and the companionship of her mother who had, for so many years, been her best friend. When

Gordon failed to spoil her the way her father had, she felt deprived. So she sought to maintain the oneness which she had always enjoyed with her parents by telephone and by frequent visits to their home. Whenever she visited them she would slip back into acting like their little girl and allow them to cosset her and spoil her.

This not only gave birth to bouts of homesickness in the early days of their marriage, it also gave rise to tensions between Doreen and Gordon. Doreen's mother was a powerful, persuasive woman. When she spoke, most people acted instantly. But not Gordon. He was determined that his mother-in-law should not be allowed to rule the roost.

Doreen's mother never intended to keep her daughter tied to her apron strings. Her love and concern for her daughter were genuine, and what she most desired was that Doreen should be happy. So when she quizzed Doreen about her relationship with Gordon, she was not consciously trying to drive a wedge between the two of them. Nevertheless, when she began to ask questions about their sex life—how often they made love, whether Doreen was enjoying a series of orgasms, whether Gordon was a sensitive lover—Doreen's concern about her marriage deepened because her mother implied that all happily married couples made love every night, and each partner brought the other to a climax. But Gordon and Doreen's pattern of love-making was not like that. Neither of them felt the need for sexual intercourse every day. And sometimes, even when they did make love, Doreen failed to experience an orgasm.

Because her relationship with her mother was so close and because she believed what her mother told her, Doreen's anxiety about her marriage changed to alarm. Perhaps theirs would be one of the one-in-three British marriages that ends in disaster! But she dared not voice these fears to Gordon because he resented the closeness she enjoyed with her mother, and he despised the way her father spoiled her as though she was still his baby girl. He would be angry if he suspected that her mother lay behind the lurking dreads and mounting tensions in their year-old marriage.

God gave me the privilege of watching him unravel this tangle. Doreen is a delightful person who set herself the task of living biblically. She came to grasp what "leaving" father and mother implies: leaving behind the dependency of childhood and becoming fully adult, leaving behind financial ties, refusing to be bound by parental attitudes and opinions and lifestyle, and creating a space around the relationship and safeguarding it with a "No Trespassing" sign. At that time, she confessed to herself, to God and to me that she had not yet "left," that she was in bondage to her parents and that this had been spoiling and endangering her relationship with her husband.

I explained to Doreen that although I do not understand fully the mystery of how God works in situations like this, what I do know is that he can snap the invisible cord that inappropriately ties an adult to his or her parents and sets a person free to live differently. Doreen expressed a desire for this ministry and so together we asked God to cut the cord which still tied her to her parents. After the prayer, Doreen testified to experiencing an unexpected but welcome sense of relief and release. She felt free to give herself wholeheartedly to Gordon.

She hurried home to explain to Gordon what had happened. She admitted that she had been making a grave mistake in putting her relationship with her parents higher on her priority list than her relationship with him, and she asked him to forgive her. She was moved by Gordon's response. He confessed the resentment he had harbored against Doreen's mother and told Doreen that he was sorry for the jealousy which had poisoned his mind. They prayed together and together received the forgiveness God delights to give. And they repented; that is, they determined to live differently.

A few days after their reconciliation they began to assess the needs not only of Doreen's parents but of Gordon's parents too. They worked out how, as a couple, they could express to both sets of parents how they loved them and wanted to establish a new relationship with each of them—a relationship which was warm and close but which did not impinge on their marriage. They enjoyed the fun of establishing how they would create a space around their marriage into which not even Doreen's mother would creep. And they enjoyed exploring a lifestyle of their own, free from the expectations of others—sexually, spiritually, domestically and in every other way.

God mended this marriage many years ago. I sometimes hear Gordon and Doreen describe the support both sets of parents give them. It reminds me again of the thread which runs, like a life-giving vein, through this book. When couples open themselves to God's wonder-working power and are obedient to the challenges he places before them, God, by his Spirit, still moves around and restores relation-ships—even those which appear to be badly ruptured.

In Doreen's case, the emotional tie which kept her in bondage to her parents was one which had once been nourishing and appropriate; it needed severing only because her parents had fulfilled their task well and now needed the generosity to let her go. Elaine's story presented a completely different example of a situation where the failure to leave was hindering the growth of a wife's relationship with her husband.

Elaine and Colin's Story

Elaine and Colin's marriage was a mess. They admitted this to my husband and me when we met them on one of the Marriage Fulfilment Weekends which we run for married couples. Elaine complained that the key to the problem lay with Colin. He was never at home. If he wasn't working or attending meetings at church, he'd be playing golf with his friends. But when we asked Colin where he understood the source of the problem to lie, his response was somewhat different. The reason he spent so little time at home, he claimed, was that Elaine never seemed pleased to see him. She gave him no affirmation or appreciation, and so he was forced to look for this outside the home. But this gave rise to complaining and bitterness from Elaine which compounded the problem.

As we talked, it transpired that Elaine's opinion of herself had always been frighteningly low. Although Colin told her frequently that she was attractive, she poured scorn on his compliments because she dared not believe them. Although he tried to show her that she was a good mother, she belittled herself and could not accept this praise either. "The problem is," she blurted out as we talked, "I feel completely unlovable. No matter what Colin says about me, I can't believe him so I push him away when he tries to say nice things to me."

When we investigated the root of this problem, we traced it back to that invisible umbilical cord which held Elaine to her mother, that tie which is as capable of conveying negative messages as positive ones. From very early on in her life, Elaine remembered her mother scolding her incessantly. Her mother insisted that Elaine was such a naughty girl that, unless she changed dramatically, no one would love her. Her father reinforced this message by spending very little time playing with her or cuddling her.

But Elaine did not know how to change. And neither of her parents helped her to see what she must do to behave differently. So she absorbed the most devastating lie of lies anyone can be asked to live with: "I am unlovable." Although she was now married and scarcely saw her parents, she still believed this untruth. It crippled her behavior and blurred her vision of herself because the umbilical cord which had fed her this poison had never been cut. In a subtle, but powerful way, therefore, her parents were preventing her marriage from succeeding because she was free neither to give love nor to receive it.

Psychologists have shown us that our deepest need as people is to know that we are loved, and that if we are denied love as children, teenagers or indeed as adults we may be robbed of a sense of well-being as well as an ability to give love and to trust those who say they love us. Psychologists have also demonstrated how deeply wounded a person can be by the kind of message with which Elaine's mother battered her in her formative years.

However, through what is called the ministry of inner healing, God has been revealing to his church in recent years that Jesus who, as the Bible tells us, is the same yesterday, today and forever, can move into these wounds of the past, heal them and draw the sting from the memories so that the memories lose their power to paralyze. Moreover, Jesus can fill with his love the inner crevices and recesses of our being which were denied the sustenance of a loving relationship.

The process of inner healing involves people first exposing the hurts of the past to the loving light of God's truth and to his healing touch, and then entrusting themselves to the ministry of God's Spirit who is capable of penetrating the depths which human words and wisdom cannot reach.

When we explained this to Elaine, a look of hope flickered into her frightened eyes, and she said she would like time to think about the implications of asking God to work in her life in this way.

Some time later, Elaine wrote to us and explained that she would like to ask Jesus to move into her painful past and change her. Would we pray with her? Could Colin come too?

During the time we subsequently spent together, God gave to my husband and me the privilege of praying that, in his name, the cord which had bound Elaine to her parents' opinions about herself for so long would be severed. We prayed that Jesus would touch and heal the pain in Elaine which had been caused because she believed herself to be unlovable and that God would shed abroad in her heart the Spirit of truth who would reveal to Elaine God's perspective of herself.

While we were praying, the sense of the presence of God was both strong and powerful. It was clear that though none of us could discern quite what God was doing, he was working in Elaine's heart gently and sensitively, tenderly and effectively.

It was while we were praying that a picture came into my mind. The picture was of a diamond. With the picture came the reminder that a diamond is formed from the darkness of a piece of coal which, when subjected to intense heat and pressure, produces the precious, priceless stone. It was as though God was using picture language to communicate that, although Elaine had been subjected to the heat and pressure of untruths for almost all of her life, nevertheless, he had produced from the darkness a jewel of very great worth. The message he wanted her to hear was that she was of unique and great value, that she was lovable.

It was while we were praying that Colin wept. It was as though, for the first time in his life, he felt part of the pain which had crippled his wife from her childhood onward. The hardness in his heart melted. He longed now to do anything in his power to underline God's truth and to show to Elaine in a whole variety of ways—through words, looks, compliments and touch—that she is, indeed, of great worth, not simply to God but to him and to their children also. And it was while we were praying that God was at work, mysteriously and powerfully healing the pain of the past and reversing its effect.

The change in Elaine has been astonishing. The anxious lines are disappearing from her face. Cautiously she is daring to look into Colin's eyes and to read there the love which he was trying hard to convey.

She has even begun to take the risk of touching him again. At first this was just a gentle stroking of the hand, but it was a beginning for two people who had almost forgotten the tenderness of touch. Set free from the cruel lies with which her mother had crushed her, Elaine was also set free to love and receive love, to learn from her husband and children the lessons she would have learned as a child had her parents given her the affirmation and affection she so much needed.

When God touches a couple as damaged as Colin and Elaine, he rarely revolutionizes their relationship so that one minute they can scarcely communicate and the next they are enjoying the romance of erotic love again. What I observed in Colin and Elaine's relationship finds a parallel in many others. The healing is a slow, ongoing process, sometimes painful in its learning and reorientation, but rich, nonetheless. It reminds me of the way the little prince and the fox discovered the wonder of closeness in Antoine de Saint-Exupery's delightful story *The Little Prince.*

Yearning for intimacy, the fox asks the little prince, who is a visitor from another planet, to tame him.

"What does that mean—'tame'?"

"It is an act too often neglected," said the fox. "It means to establish ties."

"To establish ties?"

"Just that," said the fox. . . . "If you tame me, then we shall need each other. To me, you will be unique in all the world. To you, I shall be unique in all the world."

"What must I do to tame you?" asked the little prince.

"You must be very patient," replied the fox. "First you will sit down a little distance from me—like that—in the grass. I shall look at you out of the corner of my eye, and you will say nothing. . . . But you will sit a little closer to me every day . . ."

The next day the little prince came back.

They sat a little closer to one another every day so that when it was time for the little prince to leave and return to his own country, a great sorrow seized both of them. They had learned, little by little and bit by bit, that they mattered to one another.[9]

It was with similar caution and sensitivity that Colin and Elaine found their way back to one another and the love which they had wanted to express but had been hindered from enjoying. Now that God has restored their own relationship, Colin and Elaine are trying to examine the next stage: determining what Elaine's parents' needs are now, and deciding how, despite the past, they can combine their resources and begin to meet some of those needs. And they are finding that just discussing possible ways ahead is drawing them closer together.

Steve and Joy's Story
Just as God intervened in Doreen and Gordon's marriage and Elaine and Colin's relationship, giving them the grace and ability to leave the past and parents behind, so he moved into Steve and Joy's marriage when pressures threatened to place their young relationship under unbearable stress.

Steve and Joy's wedding day is one I remember for the warmth and sincerity with which they each exchanged their marriage vows. Nevertheless, within a year, they had lost much of the sparkle which normally endears them to everyone in their circle of acquaintances and friends, and several people began to express concern for their well-being. But their problem was not that they had failed to leave their parents. Rather, it was the freedoms they had enjoyed as single people which were crowding into their "holy space" and endangering their marriage.

Both of them had lived hectic lives while they were single. Both of them held down responsible, full-time jobs and enjoyed time-consuming hobbies apart from one another. They were both deeply committed to serving God in their local church and consequently were involved in endless meetings and activities which ate into much of their free time. This was the reason why ominous cracks appeared in the structure of their relationship.

Steve and Joy are a prayerful couple who want to live life God's way. Over a period of time they began to absent themselves from services and meetings which they would normally have attended. They withdrew from various social engagements which they had previously enjoyed. Joy took a part-time job in place of her full-time one. Some months later their eyes began to shine again. Bright smiles returned to light up their faces, and they seemed full of energy and verve and love for one another once more. They explained to me what had been happening.

God had been at work convicting them that if they were to enjoy the degree of intimacy which he had designed for them, they would first have to "leave"; and that while they lived as though they were two single people sharing the same bed, leaving had not, in fact, taken place. God had underlined for them that to leave means to create a space around the relationship which no hobby and no cause, however worthwhile, might invade. To leave means to abandon former securities and familiarities so that a couple can venture into life united with the new number one: the partner in marriage. Indeed, to leave even involves a renunciation of self so that each partner is motivated not by selfish desires but by a longing to please the partner.

Steve and Joy had discovered the hard way that even though their love for the other was deep, this partner-pleasing is far from easy. Ingrained in each of us is a strong seam of selfishness. To put another before self, let alone before parents, requires self-discipline, determination and years of practice. To wake up each morning and ask not,

"How can I make myself happy today?" but rather, "How can I make my partner happy today? How can I avoid making my partner unhappy today?" goes against the grain.

And yet God, the Creator of marriage, instructs married couples "to leave": to recognize that when we marry, life must now revolve around a new number one—our partners. Where couples are taking seriously the instructions of the Maker of marriage, and where they are enlisting his help, there the world bears witness to a series of miracles, a series of marriages on the mend.

CHAPTER 3

A NEW ORDER OF PRIORITIES

THE STORY IS TOLD OF A PASTOR'S WIFE WHO, DESPAIRING OF ever finding a time when her husband would give her his undivided attention, stormed out of the parsonage and called him from the nearest telephone booth. When he answered the phone and heard her voice at the other end of the line, he was dumbfounded. But when he asked, "What d'you think you're doing telephoning your own number?" the wife replied, "It's the only way I could guarantee that you would listen to me for a few minutes. You're always so busy listening to someone else, you have no time for me." Having made her point over the telephone, she returned home.

A similar story is told of a doctor's wife who surprised her husband by arriving in his office one morning in response to the bell he used to summon his next patient. When he expressed his astonishment, his wife told him that she had been forced into playing this trick on him. It was the only way she could ensure a few moments of privacy with him.

I would find those stories funny if they did not so nearly match my own experience. Busyness besieged our own marriage on one occasion and threatened to bring about its downfall.

We had moved to a new town. The congregation which my husband was to pastor was small. Numbers had dwindled for a variety of reasons: one was because conflict had split the church down the middle. The situation was so serious that when David was first introduced to members of the church, the bishop charged them to be reconciled to one another. If they refused, the church would have to close.

David and I were not unduly daunted by this sad state of affairs. God had made it quite clear that we were to come to Nottingham. He had pledged to equip us for the task to which he had called us, and we were sure prayer had the power to change situations grimmer than this one. So we threw ourselves into the work of building up the congregation.

It seemed natural for me to work alongside David in the parish. When God had called my husband out of adult education and into the ordained ministry, he had made it clear that the call involved not only David but our entire family. Our mandate was to serve God together. So, faced with this new challenge, we worked hard willingly.

God seemed to bless the efforts we made. Week by week, people turned to Christ. Others were healed. Numbers increased. We had been warned not to expect that the extra seating area would be used again, but even that became full.

Burnt Out for God

It was not until a viral infection put me in bed for several months that I counted the cost of this seeming "success story." But as I lay there, week after week, hardly seeing my husband, I realized what was happening. We were colleagues, working alongside one another happily enough but no longer companions in the richest sense of that word. If we took a day off, we talked about "the work." At mealtimes, if the phone did not ring incessantly to distract our attention, we talked about "the work." Even in bed, it was "the work" we discussed. Consequently, at the heart of our marriage, instead of the intimacy we had once enjoyed, a cavity now yawned whose name was loneliness.

On several occasions I tried to communicate to David that our marriage was being burnt out because of our ministry and that I was frightened by what I saw happening. But each attempt proved as abortive as the last. Did the communication break down because I was aggressive in the way I tried to express my concern? Did I fail to make myself clear because David was busy doing his share of the work and mine now that I was sick? I cannot now recall why my efforts failed. What I do remember is the day when I felt so full of despair about the situation that I sat by the River Derwent in Derbyshire and longed for the courage to throw myself into its swirling waters. The emptiness seemed intolerable, and I wished I could cease to be.

It has been said that when we reach rock bottom God is there. Certainly God met us in this particular pit. The weekend after the death-wish swept over me in Derbyshire, David and I attended a conference. It was held in our own home and attended by several married couples from our parish. The aim of the weekend was to give couples an opportunity to stand back from their normal routine so that they could reevaluate their marriage at leisure. I approached the weekend with a mixture of feelings—fear and hope, pain and anticipation.

The very first talk on the very first evening seemed tailored to our own situation. The speaker warned us that, when we reach heaven, God will not ask us first to tally the number of people we had introduced into his kingdom, neither will he first ask us to list the number of prayer meetings or Bible studies we had attended. No, the first thing God will require us to do is to show if we have been faithful or foolish stewards of the marriage relationships he had entrusted to us.

I was stunned. The very thought filled me with alarm. If this claim contained even a grain of truth, both David and I would look very silly on that day when we faced our Maker. How on earth would we explain to him that frenetic activity in his name had pushed us to neglect one another and our relationship?

I longed to know what David was making of this claim. Later I found out, as together we admitted that that challenge had been aimed at us. God was exhorting us to take stock of the situation. We must make time to examine our marriage and to place it higher on our list of priorities.

A Marriage on the Mend

God once gave to the prophet Ezekiel a vision of a river which flowed from God's presence out to his people (Ezek 47). This steady stream of water contained healing, cleansing, life-giving properties. It gave life to the trees growing on the river bank. It teemed with animals and fish. When it flowed into the sea it replaced salty water with fresh water. That weekend, it was as though a tributary of that river reached our own relationship. It irrigated its parched places and made possible whole new areas of change and growth. We learned to communicate with one another in a new way; we reestablished a pattern of praying together, and our ability to express love to one another both verbally and sexually was restored. The weekend proved to be a turning-point in our battered marriage.

But some years later the emotional barrenness which is the result of busyness plagued us again. Our appointment calendars were so full that we scarcely saw one another, except at church functions. While we were abroad taking a sabbatical leave, we asked God a question: "Lord, why is our marriage under pressure again?" God gave us a direct answer to that straightforward question: "How do you expect two people like you to enjoy a relationship with one another when you scarcely see each other? If you want your relationship to grow, you must give it time—quality time." God instructed us further: "Make sure that you spend two hours together each day."

"Two hours a day. Impossible!" I took my calendar out of its case to show God just how preposterous this requirement was. Then I saw the tragedy of my own protest. I was implying that I was too busy for my husband and that I suspected he was too busy to spend time with me. God had accurately pinpointed our problem once more—not to send us on a guilt trip but rather to free us to enjoy the intimacy we both craved and for which he had given us to one another in the first place.

When God speaks as clearly as that, it is foolish to refuse to give in. We gave in. There and then we covenanted to give one another quality time every day. Whenever possible this would amount to two hours each day in addition to our days off and holidays. We knew that as soon as we returned to the parish, evenings together would be an impossibility, by and large, so we earmarked time during the day which we could spend with one another.

Marriage: The Top Priority

At first, twinges of guilt troubled us. Nottingham is full of needy people. Running a large church is a demanding task. Writing books is a time-consuming, energy-sapping occupation. Was this not a selfish use of time? Had we not been taught to "seek first [God's] kingdom" and all these things would be added to us (Mt 6:33)? Had not the word *self-sacrifice* been underlined for us all through our student days when we were growing up in the Christian faith?

God was patient with us as, step by step, he showed us that to lavish time and energy on our relationship was not a luxury but a necessity. Marriage is a vocation and though, between us, a number of vocations clamor for our attention, this vocation of marriage is our first calling. He made this plain to us from his own Word, the Bible. He took us back to that verse we began to scrutinize in chapter two: "Therefore a man leaves his father and his mother and cleaves to his wife" (Gen 2:24 RSV).

He emphasized that our over-busyness pointed to the fact that we had learned neither to leave nor to cleave. The most pressing need was that we should "leave" in the sense that we resolved to put one another first. The second most pressing need was that we should learn to "cleave" by putting that resolve into practice.

We reached for commentaries and concordances to try to tease out what this quaint word *cleave* means. We discovered that the literal sense of the Hebrew word for *to cleave* is "to adhere to" or "to be glued to" a person. Partners in marriage were to be welded together so that the two became one. But the Bible's use of this word nowhere implies a relationship which is needy, greedy, claustrophobic, wooden or restrictive. On the contrary, the relationships to which this word is applied are attractive models on which to pattern the marriage relationship. We read, for example, that Ruth "clave" to Naomi when they were both widowed (Ruth 1:14 KJV). Her request that Naomi should not ask her to leave her suggests a warm, loving, supportive relationship—a togetherness and healthy interdependence which applied equally to times of joy and times of pain, to times of stability and security and to times of change.

We also read that the men of Judah "clave" to David through thick and thin (2 Sam 20:2), implying that cleaving includes faithfulness: the desire to make the well-being of the partner in marriage a top priority.

Learning to "Cleave"

We valued David Atkinson's insights on "cleaving" in his book *To Have and to Hold*. He emphasizes that the implied faithfulness is more than a negative "putting a leash on lust," but rather the faithfulness which undergirds cleaving covers four main areas of the marital relationship.

1. Faithfulness to the marriage vow. The couple commits themselves to building the relationship on a love which outlasts eros, a self-sacrificing love which integrates affection, warmth, trust, sensitivity, reliability, stability and integrity.

2. Faithfulness to the vocation of marriage. The couple recognizes that marriage is a calling to be lived before God, a calling which is ever open to receiving his rich resources of grace, healing and forgiveness and within which the couple always works for the future growth of their partnership and its deeper fulfillment.

3. Faithfulness to the other person. Each partner dedicates himself or herself wholeheartedly to promoting the wholeness of the spouse.

4. Faithfulness to the relationship. Both partners acknowledge the permanence of their union, so both commit themselves to working at deepening their love through the good times and tough times too. And both will seek to ensure that the marriage contains all the healing properties of the parent-child relationship at its best: unconditional love, acceptance, affirmation, security and the opportunity to explore and to express oneself creatively.[10]

We realized that, though we had been married for years, we had not even begun to work at the basics of marriage: the twin arts of leaving and cleaving. But God had challenged us so clearly that we knew it was not too late to try. And he encouraged us in our resolve by showing us how other couples to whom he had given a similar challenge had risen to the occasion and, as a result, were enjoying the richness of the marital relationship at its best, even though they were busier than we were.

Yonggi and Grace Cho's Story

The first testimony which impressed us deeply was that of Paul Yonggi Cho, the pastor of the Full Gospel Central Church in Seoul, Korea. Yonggi Cho's church is both the biggest and fastest growing church in the world today. If I estimate the number of its membership, my calculation will be inaccurate by the time this book is published because that fellowship has enjoyed unprecedented growth in the past decade. But this success story also has a shadowy side.

Early on in his ministry, tensions arose in the pastor's marriage—the tensions faced by countless Christians whose zeal for God seems to be quenched by the demands the marriage relationship makes. Yonggi Cho found it all too easy to dismiss his wife's emotional needs, to write them off as "unspiritual." He protested that he ensured that she had good food, nice clothes and a comfortable home. Besides that, he was never physically violent. What more could a wife ask for? Surely it was unreasonable of her to demand that in addition, he, the pastor of a busy church, should meet her needs for companionship, love, security and value as a person! The more he thought about these needs which his wife tried to express to him, the more convinced he became that the devil was using his wife to divert him from his first calling: to win the people of Korea for Christ.

His wife, Grace, recognized that her husband was incapable of inter-
preting her needs accurately and became withdrawn. Her husband's
neglect of her through his prolonged absences from home produced an
indescribable loneliness and sense of abandonment. When he saw this
change in her, Yonggi Cho could stand the strain no longer. If the
situation grew any worse, he would have to divorce his wife. He could
not allow her to intrude on his work for God.

One day, in desperation, he prayed, "Lord, change her, or otherwise
we must separate!"

God heard that prayer and answered it, not by changing Grace Cho
in the first instance, but rather by revealing to her husband how God
required him to change. He began by showing Yonggi Cho how vital
it was that he meet his wife's needs. What kind of testimony would
he have if his wife were to leave him and he ended up divorced? His
primary role in life was not to win Korea for Christ but to love his wife
in the same way as Christ loved the church: to offer her security and
companionship and to make her whole. In other words, "to cleave."

A New Order of Priorities

God continued to deal with this man, whose passion for evangelism
seemed unquenchable, by providing him with a new order of priorities:

1. God and his relationship with him must come first.
2. Cherishing his wife was his next priority.
3. When children came along, they must come next.
4. The church came after that.

When God speaks, Yonggi Cho obeys. He reached for his appointment book, canceled certain evangelistic campaigns and began an entirely new lifestyle which included his wife. God instructed him to give
every Monday to his wife so that they could enjoy quality time together. On Mondays, therefore, they would go shopping or sit in the park

or go out for a meal together. God showed him that in Christian marriage, a man draws out his wife's full potential. He began by expressing to Grace his love and appreciation for her. In a short space of time his wife's depression lifted. Her husband's expressed love for her transformed her. Their marriage was not only mended, it became zestful. Today they are both used by God to win Korea for Christ but, under the lordship of Christ, their marriage sits on the top rung of their ladder of priorities. Everything else, including their ever-escalating pastoral responsibilities, find their pecking order after that.[11]

David Watson's Testimony

In the book of Revelation, a little sentence punctuates the second and third chapters of the book: "He who has an ear, let him hear what the Spirit says to the churches." After God had spoken to us so directly and clearly about our own lifestyle and the place our marriage should assume in it, and after reading of the way God similarly confronted Yonggi Cho, it did not surprise us to hear charismatic leader and author David Watson testify to a similar rebuke from God. For when God's heart is burdened for his people, he makes that burden plain through a variety of methods of communication.

In the last two books he wrote before his death, with characteristic humility David showed how he, too, had been convicted by God of neglecting his wife and family. When I read his testimony, I was both deeply moved and deeply burdened. It seemed as though God was aching to communicate to Christian people that he does not want them to sacrifice their marriage relationships on the altar of "serving him." He wants them, rather, to enjoy the marriage relationship so much that, under his lordship and authority, the partnership itself becomes an instrument of healing to each partner and, in turn, to others.

This realization impressed itself upon me again through another of

David Watson's testimonies. As I drove to a speaking engagement, I listened to a talk David recorded just before he died. When his final illness prevented him from personally addressing a conference of evangelists at Swanwick in 1983, he put his message on tape. On this tape, David described the burden God was laying on my own heart. David explained how his marriage nearly fell apart and how, during his illness, God had challenged him to check his priorities:

I realized that things had got out of hand and I'd been too busy. I hadn't given enough time to my wife and children. My wife had suffered an awful lot from my sheer busyness "for the Lord's sake" and I was determined to give better quality time to my wife and family if I did nothing else.[12]

Many of the evangelists hearing that resolve, I gather, were moved to tears. At least one was heard to confess that God was speaking to him through David. The man was going home to cancel some engagements so that he could give quality time to his wife and family.

The Spirit Convicts

At last, we recognized that God was not simply charging us to change our way of life to enrich our own marriage; he was winging this same challenge to Christians all over the world. My husband and I began to include teaching about leaving and cleaving in the Marriage Fulfilment seminars which we are privileged to lead. As we showed how fundamental this teaching is to the health of the marital relationship, and as we explained that these two principles are basic to Christian marriage, it sometimes seemed as though we were presenting truths which were brand new. But this teaching is not new; it is as old as marriage itself—and timeless, because it forms part of the blueprint for marriage designed by the architect of the marriage relationship, who knows best how to make it work.

The writer to the Hebrews tells us that God's Word is like a two-edged sword (Heb 4:12). It slips through our defences and prejudices and excuses, convicting us all the way. This is what we see the following verse of Scripture doing for married people: "Therefore a man leaves his father and his mother and cleaves to his wife" (Gen 2:24 RSV). And where couples act on the conviction that this verse is true, miracles are happening. God is requiring sacrifices so that marriage relationships can improve, rather than couples' sacrificing the marriage for the sake of their other pursuits.

Quality Time

When two married people donate quality time to one another, they convey several nonverbal messages: you matter to me, our relationship matters to me and I want our love to deepen with the years—not fade or die. And when a couple donates quality time to one another, both partners receive certain assurances: I am of sufficient worth to my partner for him or her to want to spend time with me, I am loved, and I am lovable. These are the most healing messages anyone in the world can hope to receive. They bring in their wake a sense of well-being. Couples who transmit and receive these messages regularly to one another and receive them from one another find that life is well worth living.

And, of course, the architect of marriage knew this when he commanded couples to leave and to cleave. And he knows that these words still hold their ancient power. That is why, when couples take his method of marriage seriously, marriages are being mended.

To continue the healing God has graciously poured into our relationship, my husband and I ask ourselves four questions whenever we are invited to take part in activities which might impinge on our marriage. The questions help us to assess whether yet another task or project will remove our marriage from the top of our priority list:

1. Will this draw us together or drive a wedge between us?

2. Will this build up our relationship or tear it down?

3. Does this express my love and loyalty for and to my partner or does it reveal my self-centered individualism or personal ambition?

4. If it requires sacrifice on the part of my partner or our relationship, is it God who is asking us to make this sacrifice with our eyes wide open or am I asking my partner to make sacrifices inappropriately?

God intends us to enjoy an inseparable union which is characterized by great joy in our togetherness. On our silver wedding anniversary, my husband and I were strolling, hand in hand, along a beach on a Greek island, and I put to him the question which was on my mind at the time: "Are you glad you married me?" When he replied in the affirmative, I asked another question: "Why? Why are you glad?" And this is what he said: "Because, even after all these years, you are my best friend."

In the silence which followed, I thanked God for the way he had mended our marriage. If I had asked those questions a few years earlier, I might have received some rather evasive answers. I looked up to the mountains which framed the beach where we were walking, felt the warmth of the sun tanning my body and heard the whistle of the wind which was playing on the waves. As I gave thanks for these signs of the grandeur of God, I gave thanks, too, for an even greater sign of his love. For this Creator God stoops down to touch us in our need, to draw married people together when life threatens to drive them apart and to perform that most moving of all miracles, the mended marriage.

CHAPTER 4

WORKING AT ONENESS

S OMETIMES GOD HEALS A MARRIAGE INSTANTANEOUSLY. ONE
minute a huge block of ice obstructs the flow of marital love.
The next minute God has dealt with the blockage and the couple
enjoys a completely new joy and ease in relating.

Sometimes, as we have seen, God heals a marriage slowly and
gradually. The way the healing comes to a couple is not unlike the
process in nature I am watching as I tramp the hills of Derbyshire while
thinking about the content of this book.

Temperatures have dropped to an all-time low—way below zero—
for weeks now. Snow covers the hills and lies, acre after acre, on the

fallow fields. Huge icicles hang, like stalactites, from the gray dry-stone walls which are the pride and joy of this part of the world. But for four days now, the sun has shone brightly for a few hours each day. And when I walk, instead of the hush which steals over the countryside when snow first falls, I am aware of an awakening. First the chirping of a robin broke in on my thoughts; next I noticed the unmistakable plop of water dripping from the nose of an icicle; then it was the distinct gurgle of running water which I heard, assuring me that the thaw had begun in earnest. Sometimes God mends marriages like that—slowly, persistently, thoroughly.

Most often God combines these two operations: mending a marriage first by intervening in a dramatic way, but then showing a couple that what he has begun, he will continue with their help. He shows them that his resources and are sufficient to match their deepest needs.

Peaks and Plateaus

This has been my husband's and my experience. We look back to occasions like the marriage weekend I described in the last chapter, and we see how God used that to change the direction of our relationship. We look back, too, to the time on our sabbatical leave when God intervened again. And I can recall other occasions when we sensed God dealing with us in equally dramatic ways.

But in between these peaks lay a series of plateaus where God laid on our shoulders the responsibility of working at our relationship for ourselves, albeit with his help.

God dealt similarly with David and Gwen Wilkerson. I related in chapter one the remarkable way in which God prevented their marriage from collapsing completely. But Gwen admits that this was not the end of the story. They relished the second honeymoon God gave them so generously and unexpectedly, and agreed that it was well worth waiting for. Gwen goes on:

By the time we had to return home we had sobered up to the point of being able to talk about our marriage objectively. Both of us recognized that the Lord had given us a new beginning as a gift, but that He expected us now to work with Him in order to keep going forward in His way. He made us acutely aware of the many mistakes we had committed in the past year—and indeed in the preceding years. We knew that these same mistakes, if left uncorrected or repeated too many times, could unravel our relationship all over again. For the first time, ever, we began to talk seriously to each other about the responsibility we shared for making our marriage work.

It frightened us both to discover how close each had been to ending our life together.

"When I left the banquet to pray, I was in such a turmoil about our relationship that I decided I'd hop a plane to Mexico and give it all up," Dave confessed. "I still am amazed that the Lord was able to bring me back."

As I digested this discomfiting bit of news, I told Dave just how determined I had been to seek a legal separation upon our return to Long Island. . . .

Then and there, we began to pray for God to shed His light on the problems we shared. The healing begun in Los Angeles was to continue for months. We had a lot of catching up to do.[13]

Most couples whose marriages have been mutilated in some way experience this marvelous mixture. They know God's presence in their marriage, yet they know, too, that years of hard work lie ahead. They know that while the love of God holds their two loves together, uniting them in a wonderful oneness, even so they have to leave, to recognize that the vocation of marriage is the most important vocation in the world. They know that they must cleave, reorganizing their timetables to make space for this top-priority relationship so that the two of them can enjoy the oneness God always intended them to enjoy.

Oneness

When a couple has learned to "leave" they are free to "cleave." And when couples have learned to leave and to cleave, they find themselves becoming one. The oneness God intended couples to enjoy contains a collection of components, including sexual oneness (which we shall examine in chapter seven of this book); social, psychological and emotional oneness (which we shall look at in the next chapter); and spiritual oneness (on which we shall focus in chapter six).

The miracle of marriage-mending often comes about because a couple touched by God determines to work at the oneness he has restored to them. Again, this was Dave and Gwen Wilkerson's experience as God pieced together the fragments of their marriage. They set aside time, at frequent intervals, for long talks about every aspect of their lives and marriage. They admit that, though it was hard work, it was well worth the effort because they were working together at their most important investment—their relationship.

Communication

Such committed communication also turned a key for my husband and me. We discovered that the secret of emotional oneness lies in the ability to communicate. On that marriage weekend we attended, we received a valuable and lasting tool for sharing with one another in depth. We learned to tell one another not just facts—"I've had a hectic day today"—but to go below the surface and to express the feelings that accompanied the facts—"I've had a hectic day today. I got through a lot of work and I feel really fulfilled." We discovered for ourselves the truth of an oft-quoted saying of John Powell's: "My emotions are the key to me. When I give you this key, you can come into me, and share with me the most precious gift I have to offer you, 'myself.' "[14]

It was strange the way this realization etched itself on our hearts. During the marriage weekend, husbands and wives were invited to write letters to one another—an invaluable method of communication perhaps introduced in England by the Marriage Encounter movement. It was while writing to David that I took the risk of exposing the real rawness inside me: the fact that I had become suicidal. I remember watching his face as he read what I had written. I remember watching the tears roll down his cheeks as my pain struck a chord in his own heart. I remember the love for him that rushed into my heart as I recognized that he was hurting because I was hurt. And I remember the reconciliation which resulted from that costly piece of self-revelation: the joy of it and the pain—pain that we had deprived one another of something as precious as deep marital love for so long.

God used that letter and the prayer time that followed to flush away the blockages which had dammed up our desire and the ability to flow together as one. God used that letter to free us to admit that oneness was what we wanted more than anything. And God also used that letter to challenge us to examine where sacrifices would need to be made so that that oneness could be restored. God showed us that, through this gift of communication, he had placed in our hands the equipment we needed to work well and efficiently and effectively together. God has never allowed us to forget that communication in relationships is vital—that when we refuse to communicate, at best our marriage stagnates and, at worst, it disintegrates.

The Value of Communication

John Powell says communication is "the lifeblood and heartbeat of

every relationship." Indeed, it is "the essential gift" of love. All other
gifts—the jewelry, colognes, flowers and neckties—are only tokens or
symbols. The real gift of love is the gift of self. He states:

Communication is the most important of all the sources of happiness and health. Communication is the essential foundation of our
happiness.[15]

When people begin to communicate effectively, a total change
begins which ultimately affects all the areas of life. The senses seem
to come alive. Color that was never noticed before is newly appreciated. Music that was not heard before becomes an accompaniment
of life. Peace that was never before experienced begins to find its
place in the human heart![16] Communication [is] the beginning of all
real change.[17]

This has certainly proved true in our own experience. That is why,
when Nick and Joy came to see me, I passed on the "secret" to them.

Nick and Joy's Story

When Nick and Joy traced for me the story of their marriage, I silently
wondered why they had married in the first place and if anything could
be done to rescue their marriage.

Everyone, it seems, had opposed the relationship when Nick and Joy
started to go out with each other. Joy's parents had objected to the
wedding, but Nick and Joy determined to go through with it, and so
they married. Now, seven years later, they were wondering whether her
parents had not been right after all. Their sex life had been a shambles
from the honeymoon onward. Their finances were completely disor-
ganized, and neither trusted the other with the management of their
joint income. There seemed to be no hobbies or interests that they
enjoyed doing together. Joy was finding the demands of motherhood
a chore rather than a challenge, so when Nick came home at night, he

returned to a whining, complaining wife rather than to the attractive, smiling girl he had married.

Nick had his troubles, too: a workload which was proving too heavy for him and a growing dissatisfaction with his colleagues. He looked to Joy for the respect, appreciation and affirmation he never received at work, but she was so absorbed in her own world of woes that she had not even recognized this need in him. Nick concluded: "I come home and go to bed early. It's a relief to be there—not for good sex but to block out a way of life which fills me with despair. Is it always going to be like this?"

I searched with them to find one strength in their relationship. If we could find that, we might be able to break into this cycle of hopelessness. But there seemed to be no obvious strengths on which to build. They no longer prayed separately, let alone together. Both were too busy, they said, to spend time with each other. The only ray of hope that I could detect was that they were adamant about one thing—they did not want to separate. They were prepared to do anything to make the marriage work. They had committed themselves to one another when they exchanged their marriage vows and, however bleak the future looked, they were determined to honor that commitment.

Since they had asked for my help, I decided to put this commitment to the test. I invited them to come back to see me again six weeks later and to use the intervening weeks to start to communicate with one another in depth. And I asked them to do this, not by talking to one another in the first instance, but by writing to one another. I suggested that they earmarked half an hour a week for this letter-writing assignment; that they refuse to go back on the resolve to give one another this half hour; and that they would use this time to respond to a series of questions which I gave them. These questions would help them divulge not just the facts of the situation ("Our marriage is in a mess") but the feelings also ("Our marriage is in a mess but I really want it to work and am prepared to work at it so that the quality of our love improves").

When Nick and Joy left me, I prayed that God would meet them in their letter-writing times, but I did not anticipate what would happen next. Six weeks later, Nick and Joy returned as arranged. When I opened the door to welcome them, I could scarcely believe the message my eyes were picking up. Nick and Joy stood there, holding hands and beaming. There was no need to ask whether the letter-writing experiment had worked—I could see for myself that a dramatic change had taken place. Later they admitted, "We're not through the woods yet, but we've taken huge steps forward. We're beginning to understand how the other feels, and we're even finding ways of meeting one another's needs."

They came to see me regularly for several months after that. Then I lost touch with them—until recently, when a letter arrived telling me that they continue to communicate in depth with one another and that, consequently, their relationship is getting better and better all the time.

The miracle of marriage-mending happened for this couple when they committed themselves to the risky task of self-disclosure. Hundreds of couples who have attended one or more of the marriage weekends which major on encouraging couples to communicate with each other would testify to a similar experience. The reason is obvious: each person who walks this earth has the need both to be accepted and understood by at least one other human being, and when couples discover that their partner in marriage is prepared to be that person, a miracle happens. The spouse who makes this discovery feels valued, loved and what the Bible describes as "known": an awareness that someone other than God is "all for you," is on your side.

Learning How to Communicate

On the desk beside me as I write stands a card which I treasure because it was once sent to me by two people whose marriage God mended. The picture shows a boy with a rake turning over some soil in the garden and a girl sitting next to him transplanting seedlings. A robin hovers over the peaceful, productive scene and alongside him the caption reads: "God lets us help when he makes miracles."

Because my husband and I have proven that to be true, and because we have seen for ourselves that good communication can benefit stressed-out as well as strong and healthy marriages, we always allocate a large part of Marriage Fulfilment Weekends to this work.

Couples coming on these weekends discover for themselves that real communication can be fun as well as rewarding. But when David and I set out on the journey of rediscovering emotional oneness through in-depth communication, we encountered certain snares. Communication, we discovered, is a complicated exchange when the people communicating are both as self-willed as we are. To communicate well and accurately does not come naturally to most of us. Neither is it an achievement which can be attained easily or automatically. So we have certain hints that we usually pass on to couples who come to our seminars. We emphasize that good communication is a two-way process, involving both conveying a message and listening to it. And we divide our hints between the "do's" and "don'ts" of conveying a message effectively and listening effectively.

Conveying Messages Effectively

Do's:

1. DO communicate the same message with your body as with your words.
2. DO watch the tone of your voice.

Communication experts tell us that the words we use compose only seven per cent of the message we convey, the tone of voice contributes thirty-eight per cent of the message and our bodily posture makes up the other fifty-five per cent. This is obvious when you think about it. A wife can greet her husband with the same words every day: "I've been waiting for you to come home." If the inflection of her voice is a whine and if she frowns or turns her back on him while she is saying it, her husband will hear her accuse him of being late or assume that the children have been disruptive yet again and his wife is requiring him to discipline them. He may well respond defensively. But if the tone of her voice is gentle and tender, if she smiles and snuggles up to him, lifting her face so that he can kiss her, he will hear a very different message. He will assume that while he has been at work his wife has missed him and is looking forward to spending time with him during the evening. He might even interpret these advances as the beginning of the tenderness which will result in physical lovemaking later that night.

Don'ts:

1. DON'T blame.

Most of us fall into this trap. Indeed, we fell into it years ago when we were children. When an adult rebuked us for intolerable behavior, we would find someone on whom to pin the blame: "It wasn't my fault. He made me do it." This practice is as old as creation itself. Adam and Eve used it when God came to them in the garden after they had disobeyed him defiantly and deliberately.

God asked Adam a direct question:

"Have you eaten from the tree I commanded you not to eat from?" The man said, "The woman you put here with me—she gave me some fruit from the tree, and I ate it." Then the LORD God said to the woman, "What is this you have done?" The woman said, "The serpent deceived me, and I ate" (Gen 3:11-13).

In other words, when confronted by God, Adam tries to apportion the blame between God and his wife while Eve pins the blame onto the serpent. Neither is prepared to accept personal responsibility for the crime they have committed. And in our communication we are often like them.

Those who wish to communicate well will replace blaming with the only alternative. Instead of accusing: "You made me mad just now," they will accept full responsibility for their own reaction and turn that sentence around so that it conveys the truth: "I was mad with you just now." It seems such a little thing but it is one of the ways we married people can help God to continue the miracle of marriage-mending which he has begun.

2. DON'T hint.

If we need the car for some reason, we must make that need known. We can't expect our partners to interpret accurately the hints we drop and to arrive at the conclusion we expect them to reach.

3. DON'T hide your vulnerability.

If we're are feeling wounded or angry, we must take the risk of exposing those feelings to our partners in some way. We can use the questions which unlock the tenderness deep down in most people: "I'm upset. Will you help me?" "I'm angry. Will you help me?"

Receiving Messages Effectively
Do's
1. DO make yourself available.

It's our responsibility to make sure our partners know we will concentrate as long as it takes to hear what they need to say. We can think of ourselves as midwives or husbands attending the birth of a first baby. We must determine to do all in our power to support our spouses as they struggle to push the message out.

2. DO listen with care. Ask yourself the questions: "What is my partner feeling?" "How can I help?" "How would he or she like me to show that I care?"

3. DO clarify.

We won't always know how to show we care. In this case, we must *ask* so that we do know what our partners need from us at any particular moment. At other times, too, when our partners are attempting to help us "walk in their moccasins," as the old saying goes—to view life as they see it—it is necessary to check out that we are picking up the same message that our partners are trying to convey. A simple enquiry every now and again is all that is required: "Do you mean? . . ." "Is this what you are saying?"

A couple I was trying to help on one occasion came to see me, and I could tell from the way they walked through my door that they had had an argument on the way to my home. In fact it turned out that they had come to tell me that the wife had decided there was no more point in working at the relationship. Living with her husband was proving impossible.

As we talked, she told me why she felt this way. She thought her husband had stopped loving her; she thought that his job mattered more to him than she did; she thought that he despised her for her faith. When I asked her why she believed these things to be true, she described to me the little signs and sentences which she had taken to point to those facts. And when I asked her whether she had ever checked out with her husband whether he really was trying to communicate these things to her, she looked even more surprised. It had not occurred to her to clarify. If she believed it, it must be correct!

One by one, we took her doubts and checked them out with her husband. To this woman's utter astonishment, her husband told her how much he loved her; that if he ever had to choose between his job and her, she would win; and that although he could not embrace Christianity for himself at that moment, he envied and admired her faith.

The wife began to smile, and I asked her how she felt about the relationship now. "It's made me realize that I do love him," she confessed. "I'd even be lost without him."

This couple is conscious that God's good hand rests on their marriage; that he brought them back together in a moving way. Even so, it will probably take years of practice before the art of good communication comes naturally to them. But they are working hard at it because, like us, they recognize that when we give time to our partners to hear what they are feeling as well as thinking, and when we commit ourselves to this task of knowing the persons we married, miracle is piled upon miracle.

The God who draws us back together with bands of love uses that time to deepen the quality of that love. And as love deepens, intimacy grows. And then an even greater miracle happens to us: we become that mysterious unit the Bible calls "one flesh." While retaining our own personality, we somehow merge with our partners to become a part of them.

I have watched this happening to a couple I have known for forty-three years. At one time they were more separate than together, divided in their opinions about a whole variety of life's problems—religion, politics, ethical issues, money, the use of the home. But now, in their later years, I see not two fiercely independent people but two who have become beautifully one.

The wife suffered an illness some months ago which left her frail, so now her husband does much of the homemaking: the cooking, the cleaning, the straightening up. Her husband, on the other hand, is deaf. When visitors come, he can only join in the conversation if she will act as his interpreter. This she does, though it is an effort for her to do so. And though they knew nothing about this book when I visited them, the wife gave me a further indication of their increasing oneness. From the cupboard by her armchair she took some Bible-reading notes. "Of course, we read these together every day now," she said with a bright smile. "It's ever so lovely doing that." They spend time together with the God who truly unites those who wait on him.

As I drove away from their home that day, I meditated on this miracle. These two, I knew, used to be one in name only. Now, elderly as they are, they are truly one: emotionally and spiritually one. And when one of them dies, through old age or illness, the sense of loss in the other will be keenly felt because, for the one who remains, one half of them really will be missing.

CHAPTER 5

NOT "I" BUT "US"

I OFTEN CONTEMPLATE THE MYSTERY OF MARRIAGE—THE WONder that, in this most intimate of all relationships, two individuals come together, entwine their lives, become one yet separate. At those times, my mind recalls a deserted beach in Cyprus which has become a favorite holiday haunt for my husband and me.

We were sauntering along that beach one afternoon in spring when an object caught my eye and captured my imagination. When I first saw it lying there, I thought it was a dead tree whose trunk had been sawn off and whose roots had been abandoned on the shore where they were now sand covered and sun scorched. But as I stooped over the mass of roots, I noticed that this was the remains not of one tree but of two. I could see where both trunks had once grown and where the roots of both trees had wound themselves around the roots of the other to form a solid, underground bond which could not be severed even in death. I remarked to my husband when he joined me, "It would take a very strong man with a very sharp ax to separate these two."

As we continued our walk, I tried to imagine how those trees had looked when they were growing in the nearby olive grove. Above ground they must have started life like any other two olive trees, growing through the sapling stage until they became sturdy, strong and well rooted. But although above ground they retained their individuality, each shaping itself to the space provided for its growth, underneath the ground something quite different was happening. These two trees were pushing their roots first toward each other and then around each other. Far from strangling each other with this intertwining of their lives, they gave one another an anchor, a security. And eventually they became, not two, but one—yet they continued to be two as well.

So far in this book we have noted that marriages are being mended where couples determine to dethrone self and take seriously the Bible's teaching on marriage: by placing the spouse and their relationship at the top of the list of priorities (leaving); by committing themselves to the support of the partner "for better, for worse" (cleaving); and by becoming emotionally one.

But as we observed at the beginning of the last chapter, the third ingredient of Christian marriage, oneness, includes a whole cluster of components. Or, to put it another way, this oneness is rather like a guitar—it has many strings to harmonize. It was always God's intention that we should enjoy the harmony and richness that oneness produces, and when couples have lost the ability to do this, he teaches them how to tune one string at a time until the instrument of their marriage is capable once more of producing pleasing sounds. This happened to Marjorie and Peter.

Social Oneness

When Marjorie and Peter told us their story, my heart ached for them. They expressed their despair in a phrase we have heard frequently: "It's the eleventh hour of our marriage." They feared that unless a dramatic turning-point could be found quickly, their relationship would be wrecked. They had been married for seven years, and although they lived under the same roof for the sake of the children, they had not really spoken to each other for five of those years. They did not want to separate, if for no other reason than the lasting hurt it would inflict on their children, but they could see no way forward.

As we talked, they described the web of negatives that held them in its grip, and we tried to help them discover a new way of cutting those threads which held them captive. They were attending the Marriage Fulfilment seminars we were conducting at the time and so had heard the Bible's teaching on leaving, cleaving and oneness. "We want to become one again, but we don't know how to start," they said.

Christian marriage is, among other things, about companionship—social oneness, enjoying the chance to do things together. Courting couples and engaged couples do this automatically. Even if their appointment books are full of other engagements, they make time to be alone together. They walk together, have meals out together, go to concerts or attend plays or watch television together. So often, married couples forget to do this, and the companionship dimension of the marriage relationship, which can be so healing in itself, withers and dies. This had happened for Marjorie and Peter. But since they were on vacation together at the time we talked, we suggested that they could begin by working at this social side of oneness. They agreed to try.

We were at Royal Week at the time. During Royal Week thousands of Christians, including whole families and fellowships, camp together on the site of the Royal Showground in Wadebridge, Cornwall. Activities are arranged for the children so parents can be assured that their offspring will not only be well looked after but will also enjoy exciting adventures at the same time. Marjorie and Peter decided that while their children attended some of these activities they would go off on their own and rediscover the wonder of the oneness which comes when two people enjoy spending time together.

Before we parted, we prayed that God would do in this couple's life the miracle they were longing to receive: a mended marriage. We arranged to meet them again on the day before Royal Week ended so that they could tell us of any changes which were taking place in their relationship. When we parted, they both seemed brighter in spirit than when they had arrived, and I noticed that these two, who claimed that they had not had a real conversation in five years, walked away holding hands—a promising sign!

The day before we were due to see them again, David and I met this couple in town. Like us, they were enjoying window-shopping in the sunshine. This time they could have passed for an engaged couple: their arms were entwined around each other and they grinned broadly when they noticed us. "By the way," the husband said, "we won't need to come to see you tomorrow as planned. God has answered that prayer for a miracle. We've found what we were looking for in one another, and we know what we have to do next. So thanks very much, but we don't need to waste any more of your time."

As I walked away from Marjorie and Peter that day, I thought of an author I once met at a booksellers' conference. This man owns a guitar, but unlike most guitars, his boasts four strings, not the normal six or twelve. Yet he plays it well; his tunes are not only recognizable but pleasing to hear and his harmonies make a delightful accompaniment for the songs he sings to vast audiences of children. Peter and Marjorie had tuned two strings on the instrument of intimacy, so far as I could tell: the string of social oneness and the string of commitment to the marriage. It was not much, but it was a significant beginning. God would take them on from there to tune other strings of their relationship. Then they would rediscover the joy of lives which meet and touch to produce the oneness which deep down they both long for.

In his book *A Severe Mercy*, Sheldon Vanauken pinpoints the importance of the kind of oneness Marjorie and Peter were rediscovering:

"Look," we said, "what is it that draws two people into closeness and love? Of course there's the mystery of physical attraction, but beyond that it's the things they share. We both love strawberries and ships and collies and poems and all beauty, and all those things bind us together. Those sharings just happened to be; but what we must do now is share everything. Everything! If one of us likes anything, there must be something to like in it—and the other one must find it. Every single thing that either of us likes. That way we shall create a thousand strands, great and small, that will link us together. Then we shall be so close that it would be impossible—unthinkable—for either of us to suppose that we could ever recreate such closeness with anyone else. And our trust in each other will not only be based on love and loyalty but on the *fact* of a thousand sharings—a thousand strands twisted into something unbreakable."

Our enthusiasm grew as we talked. Total sharing, we felt, was the ultimate secret of a love that would last for ever. And of course we could learn to like anything if we wanted to. Through sharing we would not only make a bond of incredible friendship, but through sharing we would keep the magic of inloveness. And with every year, more and more depth. We would become as close as two human beings *could* become—closer perhaps than any two people had ever been. Whatever storms might come, whatever changes the years might bring, there would be the bedrock closeness of all our sharing.[18]

The Bible, too, highlights the importance of this social oneness. It is hidden in an important verse in the first book of the Bible, where we read how God conceived the concept of the marriage relationship: "The LORD God said, "It is not good for the man to be alone. I will make a helper suitable for him" (Gen 2:18).

Sin had not yet polluted the world. Adam's surroundings were absolutely perfect. Yet Adam was weighed down by loneliness until God created a companion for him. This is only reasonable; God had made Adam in his own likeness—that is, ready for relationships. In the absence of relationships, even Adam's health was under threat, so God made him "a helper" in the form of a wife.

The Hebrew word for *helper*, I am told, carries a variety of meanings. It means, among other things, a person who assists another to reach complete fulfillment; a person who comes to the rescue of another; a person qualified to complete or correspond to another by providing the missing pieces from the puzzle of the other's life. In other words, a helper is a stimulating companion at every stage of life's journey. This word *helper* is never used of an inferior. Indeed, very often, the word *helper* is used of God himself. So we read the psalmist's joyful testimony: "God is my helper . . ." (Ps 54:4, RSV).

Peter and Marjorie were experiencing one facet of this companionship: social oneness. When God restored to them this closeness, they were reexperiencing the joy of living interlocking lives. Gradually the seemingly unbridgeable gulf between them was narrowing. In short, God was giving them the joy of saying "we" instead of "I," and "us" instead of "me"—a joy which had bypassed them for years.

Sensitive Oneness: Martin and Diana's Story

Martin and Diana's relationship had fallen apart, not because they spent too little time together but because they were in each other's company too much. Both were out of work when they married. In place of the fulfilling work each had been engaged in before their wedding day, they now found that time dragged. They had moved to a new area almost as soon as they married. The apartment they lived in seemed pitifully small and inadequately furnished. All these circumstantial factors added pressure to the normal readjustment phase of marriage. Even so, their hopes for their relationship were high and, determining to work at intimacy, they did everything together. They ate breakfast together, did the dishes together, prayed together, went shopping together, went to church together and always went to bed at the same time as the other.

Diana loved this togetherness—so much so that she dreaded the day when Martin would find employment and would have to spend part of his day away from her. However, this high degree of togetherness imposed a strain on Martin. It was not that he did not love Diana nor that he no longer wanted to spend time with her. He simply yearned for space to think his own thoughts from time to time, a place where he could say his own prayers and, ideally, a den to which he could retreat now and again to carry out do-it-yourself jobs or simply "to be." Even the freedom to walk the streets on his own without his wife in tow would help. But in the absence of this space from Diana, the pressure built up inside him. Quarrels erupted and increased in frequency and violence before God stepped in and mended the fractured marriage. His instrument of healing for this marriage was a counselor who showed both Martin and Diana the value of sensible, sensitive oneness.

By sensitive oneness I mean the mature, relaxed oneness where both partners recognize that their spouse's needs frequently differ from their own. One, like Diana, may relish the company of others for most of the day; the other, like Martin, might love people so long as he can escape from them from time to time. One, like Diana, might value shared prayer; the other, like Martin, might appreciate praying with others so long as his private devotions can be safeguarded also.

Sensitive oneness occurs when both partners place their own needs alongside those of their spouse so that both sets of needs can be met. Sensitive oneness only occurs in couples who trust one another sufficiently to experiment with varying degrees of togetherness and varying degrees of time spent apart.

Because Martin and Diana are both resilient people and eager to learn new ways of behaving, they were able to work out a timetable which fulfilled Diana's longing to spend the majority of her time with Martin and Martin's need to be with Diana for part of the day but to be alone at times too. They decided that while Martin spent some much-needed time on his own, Diana would make new friends with those people in the church she would like to know better.

They also opted to spend time regularly with a counselor who would help them make some of the adjustments every married couple must make as two innately sinful people seek to create a mutually supportive relationship.

Through this counselor, Diana discovered that not everyone welcomes the kind of closeness she was demanding from Martin. Indeed, for some people, such a high degree of togetherness feels like an invasion of their entire personality rather than an assurance of love. She also discovered that to demand a loved-one's constant presence can stem from immaturity instead of love. A child will eventually learn to play happily in nursery school, apart from his mother. This happens when that child has acquired a sufficient degree of trust and has internalized his mother's love, which results in knowing that being loved does not depend on his mother's presence.

Similarly, spouses have to learn to internalize their partners' love so that the need to cling to them possessively diminishes. They must know that just as their love is inside them, so their partner's love is real, whether they are together or apart. When Diana realized this she asked God to increase her ability to receive her husband's love and to trust in it even when he was not with her.

At the same time, God used the counselor to help Martin see his innate selfishness which used "a need for space" as an excuse to avoid working at closeness with people—including his wife. He repented of this attitude and asked God to give him the resources he needed to meet Diana's needs more adequately: the willingness to sacrifice time for her, to understand her different needs and to meet them.

The result was a degree of healing for both Martin and Diana. Both were purged of the scourge of selfishness. Diana came to demand less of Martin's time, and Martin began to offer his wife more time.

A friend of mine once diagrammed for me the richness of this sensitive oneness which balances a couple's need both for togetherness and space. What he drew is shown on page 80, and it describes the relationship which Martin and Diana now enjoy. There are times in life when husband and wife move along at the same pace, enjoying a variety of activities with one another. In the diagram, these times are shown by the two arrows running downstream and side by side. Equally, there will be times when one partner or the other will explore tributaries apart from the spouse. These are represented by the arrows going off at a tangent before returning to the mainstream once more.

In good, vital relationships, the couple will spend many hours

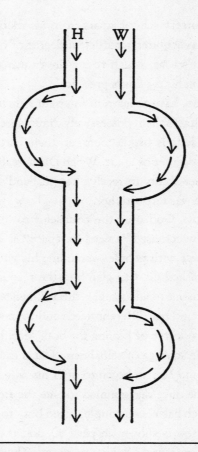

Shared lives and separate lives in succession, adequately meeting the needs of both partners.

relaxing together, or caring for their home or family together, or enriching their relationship through prayer together, or deepening their understanding of one another through communicating and listening. But they will also spend an agreed amount of time apart: working at their careers, enjoying certain hobbies, meeting friends, working at certain projects on their own. In a growing relationship, these solo explorations, far from being detrimental to the relationship, will enhance it because the spouses each return from their chosen occupations enriched, exhilarated and prepared to offer their marriage the wealth of learning gained while apart. The horizons of both expand. Each individual matures. And the marriage gains momentum as each tributary feeds the flow of that lovely friendship which is marriage.

Crisis Closeness: Graham and Margaret's Story

Graham and Margaret's relationship had not broken down or failed its efficiency inspection. But it was carrying a load which it seemed ill-equipped to bear: Graham and Margaret longed for a baby. For seven years they hoped to conceive and for seven years nothing happened. Perhaps only other childless couples who long for children can appreciate fully the subtle pressure this exerted on the relationship. There were emotional tensions which threatened to divide the two of them and spiritual blockages which added to the stress. Relationships with others piled pressure upon pressure. And Margaret, who was still emotionally immature, alarmed her husband by her over-dependence on him. She seemed to cling to him like a frightened child. Margaret once tried to express to me the kind of feelings which upset her equilibrium month by month:

I think one of the greatest problems was the monthly cycle—me getting very tense and irritable towards the end of the month and less tolerant with Graham and everybody else. The big thing was the fear of the period coming on—getting worried about it beforehand and then getting angry when it did. I would usually be terribly upset for several days before I could come down to earth again. We found it extremely difficult to see where God's love was in all this. We felt very rejected, and we couldn't bring God into the problem. We couldn't pray about it constructively, and we wanted to avoid situations where there were couples with young children.

The crisis threatened to pry them apart. It left them feeling isolated and aroused constant anxiety. As Graham explained to me, he found the monthly cycle hard, as well, in that he was faced with the challenge of coping with Margaret's ups and downs. He didn't know from one month to the next how to react to certain situations, because he could never predict how these situations would affect his wife.

"I found this really draining, from time to time," he recalled. "The question each month was: Would God do this thing we had asked for? Every new event in our lives became a major hurdle as we wondered whether this change would bring on the pregnancy: my change of job, a holiday, the move to a new home."

They found it difficult to share the problem with others. "People didn't understand and often made tactless comments," Graham told me. "We therefore decided it was a taboo subject: not something we wanted to talk about to anybody but our closest friends."

They went for medical help, but the treatments added trauma to the situation. "Emotionally it was upsetting and this resulted in sexual tensions between Margaret and myself and spoiled our sexual relationship."

Perhaps the biggest strain was that the problem refused to go away. "Wherever we went, there was always this big black cloud hanging over us," Graham told me. This was detrimental to their spiritual relationship. Graham found it difficult to understand why Margaret blamed God for the problem—and told him so.

Joy Laced with Pain

God intervened for these two people whose ability to trust one another was being so sorely tested. The pain which threatened to pry them apart resulted, instead, in drawing them closer to one another. This happened in two ways: first, because few friends outside the situation could empathize with Margaret and Graham's bleak situation, the couple was thrown back on one another. And second, because they worked hard at supporting and understanding one another in the pain, they were drawn closer together. As Margaret put it: "It brought a bond. Love was enriched and deepened."

But God broke into the relationship in another way to complete this work of marriage-mending. As the years passed and the absence of any sign of a child of their own pushed them to apply to adopt a child, Margaret's bitterness toward God increased and so did their feelings of rejection by God. In this vital matter, God seemed not to care.

Yet God did care. And he acted. As Graham admits: "The Lord led us to places and people where help and counsel were given, so even through the trauma people undertook to pray for us." And God honored those prayers by bringing healing to Margaret in a way neither of them expected.

When she received counseling on one occasion, God helped her to disentangle the threads of her thinking. There were two problems here, not one. The first was childlessness; the second, the anger she felt toward God for not granting her her heart's desire: a baby. They dealt with the second first and discovered that this anger sprang from a pain whose root was much longer than the infertility problem. It stemmed way back into her childhood, in her relationship with her father. Margaret recalled how she had always felt rejected by her father, sensing that he had love to spare only for her brother and that there was none left for her—the mere girl. Because of the insecurity this lack of self-worth engendered, she projected onto God the characteristics she detected in her earthly father and persuaded herself that, although God cared for and accepted everyone else she prayed for, his acceptance excluded her.

Through the ministry of inner healing with the laying on of hands, God met Margaret in this childhood pain. As she explains it: "He took me back to all the hurtful parts of my past and really did heal them so that I knew that I was loved and accepted right from the beginning." This healing of the emotions and renewal of the mind sent ripples through the entire relationship. Margaret experienced a new joy and freedom as a person. As her sense of security in God increased, she had less need to lean so heavily on Graham and therefore grew in maturity. As Graham detected the change in his wife, the level of trust and hope in him rose. So the crisis which had threatened to divide them resulted instead in bringing about a wonderful mending of their marriage. Instead of witnessing the death of marital intimacy, they watched it spring to new life.

Emotionally they were closer to one another than ever before and, since emotional intimacy is the foundation on which all other intimacies are built, this paved the way for satisfying sexual intimacy, genuine spiritual intimacy and that special degree of creative intimacy which comes to those who witness God deeply at work in their lives and relationships. Margaret and Graham now express this creative intimacy by leading a house group together in their church and by helping other couples and individuals who seem to be living under a dark cloud similar to the one which used to threaten to engulf them.

When Margaret and Graham told me their story, my mind flashed back to some words I wrote in *Two into One*:

Some of the richest marriages are those that have worked their way through disasters that would have shattered others, but because they refused to give up and worked towards a solution in partnership *with* God, they reached a maturity and a joy they had never imagined possible.[19]

Because they worked their way through the darkness, Graham and

Margaret discovered hidden treasures, not least in the thousand sharings which now hold their marriage together.

God is breaking into the lives of married people and drawing together the threads of their lives through a whole cluster of onenesses. He continues to do that for my husband and me. As we share mind-stretching experiences, such as reading a life-changing book or attending a conference and discussing its contents, the result is a genuine touching of our minds, a growing mutual respect for one another. This intellectual oneness draws us close to one another.

When together we attend a fine concert, or watch a well-choreographed ballet, or contemplate the wonder of God's creation in nature, in that aesthetic oneness we recall that the oneness we so nearly lost can constantly be quickened by God if we give him the chance. And that special oneness which comes from sharing certain tasks with another—homemaking, gardening, caring for others—ignites within us the spark of love which makes married life worth living.

Perhaps that is why these olive trees in Cyprus seemed so appealing. Just as their roots groped toward one another almost instinctively, bringing about a unity which did nothing to stifle the trees' individuality, so God is producing that kind of growth in our relationship. It is slow. It is gradual. It is fun. And it is summed up beautifully by some words written by my friend John Sayers:

> To
> two
> who
> became one
> and
> the one
> which was
> far greater

than
the two
ever were
for
they were joined
by Another
and became
complete
and
wholly
HIS

CHAPTER 6

MENDED THROUGH PRAYER

ALFRED LORD TENNYSON ONCE MADE THE CLAIM THAT "MORE things are wrought through prayer than this world dreams of." For the purposes of this book, perhaps I may be permitted to paraphrase that famous saying and to reword it in this way: More marriages are being mended through prayer than most Christians dream of.

In his letter to the Christians in Rome, the apostle Paul helps us to understand why these are not extravagant claims but rather that we can expect dramatic answers to prayer. He emphasizes that the same power which raised Jesus from the dead indwells Christians today: "the Spirit of him who raised Jesus from the dead is living in you" (Rom 8:11).

In other words, as Christians, we have power at our fingertips. We have within us resources of power which can break into a needy world, but this power is barricaded behind barred gates. A hand must slide back the bar so that the creative energy of God can do its work. The hand that releases the same power that once rescued Jesus from death's clutches is prayer.

A remarkable answer to prayer took place while I was preparing to write this chapter. As I mentioned in the preface, I have come away to a cottage in the country to write this book. But my husband and I meet regularly as well as keep in touch by telephone. Two evenings ago, my husband drove out from Nottingham to spend the evening with me. And I prepared a meal for us to enjoy curled up together by the log fire. While I was serving this meal, I touched one of the burners of the stove, not realizing that it was on. Three fingers of my left hand were badly scorched. I held my hand under cold water for several minutes but the pain refused to go away.

Later that evening, friends joined us. While we were chatting with them, I grew increasingly anxious about my hand. It was still hurting and telltale blisters were appearing on the three fingers. As usual, I was working against the clock, and I knew that I would need those fingers the next day if I was to continue typing.

Before our friends left us, we prayed together. During the course of this prayer, they asked God to touch my hand and heal it. The prayer was simple enough: "And please, Lord, you know that Joyce needs those fingers for typing tomorrow, so make the skin come completely clear by the morning."

I think all of us must have been aware of the sense of the presence of God which filled the tiny lounge while we prayed. Certainly I was. Perhaps it should not have surprised me, then, that while my friends were putting on their coats to leave, the pain left my hand for the first time in five hours. I slept soundly that night, and next morning when I examined my fingers there was no sign of a single blister—just a scorch mark on two fingers, perhaps to remind me that the burn had really happened and was not just a bad dream.

The power that healed my hand that night also heals hurting marriages. Prayer unleashes this power. Prayer changes situations. Prayer changes people. Prayer swings open the door through which Jesus walks to center stage from the wings of our lives. And where Jesus is, there is power and compassion and creative, effective, efficient healing.

Jesus says, "Here I am! I stand at the door and knock. If anyone hears my voice and opens the door, I will come in and eat with him, and he with me" (Rev 3:20). The writer to the Hebrews says that Jesus is praying for us continually. What these verses imply is that, while we are hurting, Jesus is praying and caring and longing to be invited into the hurting, hopeless situations so that he can deal with them. And marriages are being mended where people are taking Jesus at his word; where they are using the "open sesame" of prayer to bring about the miracle which takes place when heaven's resources touch earth's needs and meet them. Indeed, it is the message of this entire book that, in terms of needy marriages, this touch of heaven has not lost its ancient power nor is it less available today than of old. It is there. God wills us to avail ourselves of it.

Some Results of Prayer

I make that claim because almost all the couples I have mentioned in this book so far enjoy mended marriages today because someone undergirded their disintegrating relationship with costly, committed prayer. I think of Richard and Sally, whose marriage I referred to in chapter one. Their relationship was on the rocks. Divorce proceedings were well under way. But Christians were praying for them. And the power of God did for Richard and Sally what they were unable to do for themselves: It brought them into a new and vital relationship with one another which now benefits them, their family and countless others.

Or I think of Bob and Pat, the farmer and his wife I also mentioned in chapter one. While Bob searched for God, a friend prayed. The result of that caring prayer was another transformed marriage. And as I reflect on our own marriage and the manner in which God turned the tide for us so dramatically and unexpectedly, I see that the same principle applies. As I have said, the turning point came one weekend when we attended a conference for married couples. Throughout that entire weekend, two busy professional people were holding our relationship up to God in prayer. They knew none of the details I have described in this book. But they prayed. And God mended our marriage.

This phenomenon occurs too frequently for it to be dismissed as coincidental. Sometimes the person whose prayer provides the bridge on which human pain and supernatural healing meet is a bystander; a concerned, caring, compassionate friend or acquaintance of the couple. Sometimes the person whose prayer unlocks the gate of heaven is one of the spouses locked in conflict. It was Pastor Yonggi Cho's own prayers which brought about the change in attitude which led, in turn, to the mending of his marriage. And it was the combined prayers of David and Gwen Wilkerson, offered separately and born of desperation, which released the catch and let loose the power of God which rescued their marriage from certain demise.

Just as God answered these prayers for marriages in the public eye, so he is answering similar prayers uttered by couples whose names will never hit the headlines.

More Miracles

I think of a woman I once met when I presented a daylong seminar about Christian marriage. During the final session of this conference, I attempted to answer questions which had been placed in the question box provided. One of the questions I found there read: "How do you make a Christian marriage if your husband is not a Christian?" I admitted in my reply that the short answer to that question is that you cannot do it. It takes two Christians to make a *Christian* marriage. That is why the Bible places an embargo on marriages contracted between believers and unbelievers.

"Nevertheless," I suggested, "I believe that the responsibility of those who are married to non-Christians is to bring on board the ingredients of Christian marriage and work them into the recipe of their relationship, trusting God for the outcome. But it will be hard. It's hard enough when *both* partners are Christians. When one is not yet a believer, it is doubly hard. Perhaps those of us who are married to Christians should covenant to pray for those who have the uphill task of living with a partner who does not yet believe."

A year later, I was invited to return and to address the same group of people at another daylong conference. I was about to load books into my car at the end of the day, when a woman approached me. Shyly she asked, "Could I have a word with you, please?"

"I wanted to encourage you," she continued. "Last year, I was at that day conference when you told those of us with non-Christian husbands to live biblically. Well, I did that. I really tried hard. I tried to show my husband that he was number one in my life. I cooked him his favorite meals. I did everything you said. And I prayed hard. About three months after the conference, my hubby started asking all these questions about God. Then he started coming to church with me. And then he became a Christian, and now we've got a brand-new marriage.

I thought you'd like to know so that you can tell others that it really does work."

Maureen had to pray for much longer than three months before her husband, Les, turned to Christ. Les, a professional rugby player, prided himself on being a man's man. Rugby was his whole life. For him it was the most thrilling thing in the world. On the day he won a cup final medal at Wembley, this was how he felt: "It was an absolutely fantastic experience. I never thought that there would be anything that could ever come close to how I felt that day when I climbed the steps to the royal box to receive my medal."

But Les and Maureen's marriage was far from "fantastic." While Les's dreams for himself came true, and while he spent his time with his friends in the nearby pub or at the local working men's club or off fishing on his own, Maureen stayed at home bringing up their two boys on *her* own.

After Maureen was found by God, she experienced such a wealth of joy that she wanted Les to experience this too and so she began to pray for him. But Les showed no signs of giving his life to God. On the contrary, Maureen and her boys had to coerce Les to attend the annual carol service with them and then had to listen to his complaints about the service all the way home. And one year, Les thought the vicar was criticizing him personally when he referred, in his sermon, to "blokes who try to live up to the image of the Tetley Bitter Men"—the British equivalent of the tough guys you'd see on a Budweiser commercial or a Marlboro ad. Les swore he would never darken the doors of the church again. But Maureen continued praying.

Her prayers seemed to bear no fruit until Les was threatened with being laid off. This normally happy-go-lucky man suddenly crumbled. Here was a situation totally outside his control. He knew he could not sort this problem out for himself. "So one night, driving home down the motorway, I just asked God to do it for me. It was as simple as that—no fuss. I got home and had my tea on my own—Maureen and the boys were out for the evening. Then, as I wasn't sure that God had heard me, I got down on my knees by the chair and asked him to come into my life again. That's when I felt this lovely warm feeling that was even better than being at Wembley. From that time I've never looked back."

Two days later, Les told Maureen about this conversation with God. Although she had been praying for this moment for years, she could not believe that Les had at last handed over the controls to God until he, rather sheepishly returned the following Sunday to the church he had vowed he would never again attend.

Les changed. And as he changed, life in the family changed. As Maureen remembers it:

He used to think that if ever he took us all out anywhere he was really doing us a favor and deserved to have another night out as some kind of reward. Now we really enjoy spending time together. We have a whole different outlook on life.

And as Les puts it:

We didn't mean it to happen, but we were just drifting. Even when I had nights in, I'd just watch the TV. I didn't realize it at the time, though. I thought that my life was pretty good. Sundays I'd get up early and go fishing, then come back while they were still out at church and be washed and out down the club before they got back. Then I'd come home about three o'clock P.M., have lunch and fall asleep for the afternoon. . . . I just wish I'd realized so much sooner there was more to life than that.

Spiritual Oneness

But Maureen's joy did not end with her husband's conversion. Just as prayer brought her and her husband together in a miraculous way, so their growing spiritual oneness cemented their relationship.

It was fantastic for me after all those years of praying for him. We used to sit up until two or three A.M. just talking together and reading our Bibles. We hardly got any sleep for weeks, but we didn't mind because we were so excited.[20]

Like the other onenesses we highlighted in previous chapters: emotional oneness, social oneness, sensitive oneness, crisis oneness, intellectual oneness and creative oneness, God mends marriages through spiritual oneness. Sometimes, as we have seen, this oneness comes as a gift from God in answer to prayer. But sometimes the spiritual oneness which the couple creates as they pray for one another and with one another and against the enemy is the tool God uses to mend a marred marriage.

Paul and Jenny heard me make this claim at a Marriage Fulfilment seminar and they were soon to discover the truth of this statement for themselves.

Jenny described her marriage to Paul as a "noncommunicating marriage." Since both Paul's mother and Jenny's mother were strong, dominating women, Paul resolved even before he and Jenny married that he would be the boss of the marriage. He had no intention of allowing his wife to dictate to him in anything.

In practical terms this meant that after they were married, when Jenny wanted to discuss matters of pressing importance like birth control, or household care, or the discipline of their children, Paul would cut her short and refuse to talk. Paul had decided that they would start a family straightaway and so there was no need to talk about contraception. When the children were growing up, he decided what punishment, if any, should be meted out to them when they were naughty. Jenny recalls, "Even though he had read through the books on marriage, nothing hit him that his attitude of superiority and his total disregard of my need to communicate was really important."

But, during the Marriage Fulfilment seminars, God challenged him. He underlined for Paul the importance of cherishing his wife, which involved giving her time to talk and to share and to pray with him. At the same time, God convicted Jenny of the fierce independence which had prevented her from putting her husband first. As a result, Paul and Jenny determined to carve out a time each week which they would devote to one another. During this time, among other things, Jenny would unload some of the fears and anxieties she harbored about the children, and Paul would begin to learn the difficult art of communicating in depth. Having shared concerns and joys with one another in this way, they would commit them to God in shared prayer.

I can still remember the joy which lit up Jenny's face when she confided in me that through the emotional and spiritual oneness which followed this resolve, the rift which had scarred this relationship for years had been completely healed by God. She and Paul were more one than they had ever been. And when I asked permission to use their story in this book, Jenny's response was generous: "If hearing about the healing God poured into our marriage could encourage other couples to open themselves to a healing touch from God, then, of course, it must appear within the pages of your book."

Perhaps it should not surprise us that, when a couple prays together, miracles happen. It is not just that, as the old maxim claims, those who pray together stay together. There is a stronger reason why wise couples cultivate a spiritual oneness. It is this: Jesus once promised that where two or three people meet in his name he is especially present. For centuries, married couples seem to have ignored this verse, failing to recognize its significance for them. But where couples like Paul and Jenny are not only recognizing the potential hidden in this promise but are also acting on it by seeking God together, they find that there, right in the middle of their relationship, God is. His presence is as real and relevant to them as it was when God talked with the first married couple he created way back in Genesis.

Praying with Each Other

My husband and I used to find it difficult to pray together, but the more healing God pours into our marriage, the more we discover the value of the three dimensions of spiritual oneness:

1. Praying with one another
2. Praying for one another
3. Praying against the enemy

I determined to reach the root of the problem and discover why I felt embarrassed to pray with the person who is both my husband and my closest friend. When I asked God to show me the reason for this seeming inconsistency, I was surprised by what he showed me. The problem lay, not in our spirituality, as I had feared, but in our personalities. David is an extrovert. Extroverts, people who like to reach outside of themselves for their resources, like to pray aloud using a stream of words which seem to bubble out of them effortlessly. But I am an introvert. Introverts are often private people who find their resources, including their spiritual resources, inside themselves. Introverts prefer silence to noise. In prayer they dispense with words because words seem inadequate to express the sentiments which they long to express to God.

One partner, it seemed, liked to use words in prayer. The other preferred to dispense with them because words trivialized what they were trying to express. The problem was as simple and as complex as that. And it had dogged us for years. It had never occurred to us to pray together in silence. The only pattern of shared prayer we had ever learned was verbal prayer: two people coming together and saying words out loud to God. Now that God had put his finger on the problem, we decided to experiment with new methods of praying together.

In the early days the effect of this experiment was that when we prayed together, David would pray aloud while I would remain silent. Although, in one sense, we were both happy with this, now that we understood one another more completely, it seemed more like a compromise than a solution to the problem, so we made further experiments. We were learning that no one person can claim simply to be an introvert just as no one person can be described as an extrovert through and through. A mixture of these two extremes is to be found in everyone, and one sign of wholeness is that the extrovert will learn to be in touch with the introverted side of his or her personality just as the introvert will learn to give expression to the extroverted side of his or her nature. So if I was to grow in wholeness I, the introvert, could learn to pray using words spontaneously, the way my husband does. He, in turn, could learn the richness of silence.

It worked. And the result has been a varied diet of prayer which we both appreciate. Now we pray together most days just before our midday snack. Sometimes one of us will pray aloud. At other times we agree to pray silently. As we hold hands, we lift our marriage and our home, our children and our work, to God in wordless prayer. And time after time, we experience the fulfillment of that promise made by Jesus: we sense his presence by our side, right there at our meal table.

Charlie Shedd, a Christian marriage counselor who has himself enjoyed forty years of fulfilling marriage, advises couples simply to link hands and to pray together silently at the end of the day. Where couples known to me are doing this—joining hands, watching an action replay of the day, thanking God for every sign of his love to them and lifting their relationship to God in trusting, childlike prayer—their marriages, like Paul and Jenny's, change, becoming more mature and whole. And as they give God access to the scarred parts of their marriage, he mends them.

Praying for Each Other

But praying with one's partner, while being a vital ingredient of spiritual oneness, is only one ingredient. Quite as important is a parallel discipline: praying for one's partner. God underlined for me the importance of this privilege while he was busily bringing together the fragmented remains of our own relationship. He showed me one day that, though the list of people for whom I prayed was long, my husband's name was not on it. "Pray for him every day," God seemed to say.

When I protested that prayer was a time-consuming occupation, God seemed to show me that there were many minutes of every day which I was wasting: times when I would be performing menial tasks which require little thought, such as washing dishes, ironing, brushing my hair, brushing my teeth. "Use one of these times to pray for David," God's voice seemed to insist. So I did—and the change in our relationship astonished me. It was not that anything in the relationship changed—what changed was me. And when I stopped to think, this was hardly surprising.

Prayer at its best takes place when the person at prayer focuses fully on God and becomes aware of his holiness and his omnipotence. When that person intercedes for another in the way God was challenging me to pray for my husband, the person at prayer continues to focus God but at the same time seeks to identify with the feelings of the person being presented before God's throne. If that person is hurting, the person at prayer may identify with some of that hurt. If the person being prayed for is celebrating, the person at prayer may be washed with some of the spray of that joy. And if the prayer is authentic, something even more profound will happen. The person at prayer will then pause to listen for any instructions God might give to show the one praying how to become, at least in part, an answer to the prayer. So while this prayer might do little to change the nature of the relationship between husband and wife, it might change the one praying so dramatically that the whole direction of the marriage changes.

I knew this miracle was happening to our relationship when David was in inner turmoil on one occasion shortly after the marriage weekend I have described. Someone had let David down badly, and as a result a young couple expecting their first child was faced with homelessness. While I was praying for David that morning, I sensed, at one and the same time, the compassion of God and the pain which was paralyzing my husband. God's instructions to me that day were: "You be the channel through which my tenderness and understanding, holding love flows freely." Having received my instructions, I went into David's study where I found him slumped in his chair, weeping. At first I sat with him, quite silently. It seemed enough. Then, as we talked and prayed together about the crisis, I knew that God was using me to be an instrument of healing to my husband. I also knew that through this prayer we were being drawn closer together with bands of unbreakable love.

Praying Against the Enemy
Wherever God is at work mending battered relationships, Satan is at work also, seeking to destroy God's handiwork. Several letters on my desk remind me of that fact: couples who, having experienced a touch of God on their relationship, find themselves hemmed in on every side by discouragements, often of a practical nature. A couple decides to

work at the social side of their relationship. They go on vacation together only to find that the children come down with a virus. They spend most of their vacation cleaning up the children's vomit and then return home to discover that the furnace broke down while they were away and in the freezing conditions of February in England their pipes have frozen solid.

While some of these hazards are normal—the rough and tumble of family life which we must expect—some of it stems from Satan himself who delights to stir up trouble when couples' marriages are being mended by God. This happens, in particular, to couples whose marriages are on the front line for God, usually those involved in Christian leadership. The attack often seems vicious. It leaves the couple terrified that their relationship is doomed.

This happened to two friends of mine. I was praying for them on one occasion and seemed to see them being consumed by fierce flames which licked their faces and refused to die down. When I asked God for the meaning of this picture, I sensed that he was telling me that this couple was under attack and that I was to pray.

A few hours later, I talked to this couple and they told me a little of what had been happening in their lives. God had been using them richly: Through their ministry men and women were turning to Christ and through their counseling others were being healed. But their marriage seemed to be in serious trouble. Nothing had seemed capable of helping this couple. Counseling had left them as confused as before; talking things through had resulted in further emotional tangles and prayer seemed to have lost its power.

Eventually, light had broken into their darkness. Someone had helped them put two and two together and recognize that this was a backlash from God's enemy for the magnificent ministry God had been able to exercise through them. As soon as they discerned this, they knew how to pray. In the same way that Jesus sent Satan packing when the serpent sidled alongside him in the wilderness, they stood on the authority of the name of the Lord Jesus Christ, resisted Satan and commanded him to leave their marriage. And Satan went.

But he will return, as the apostle Peter reminds us: "Your enemy the devil prowls around like a roaring lion looking for someone to devour" (1 Pet 5:8). And as Paul underlines: "For our struggle is not against flesh and blood, but against the rulers, against the authorities, against the powers of this dark world and against the spiritual forces of evil in the heavenly realms" (Eph 6:12).

Satanists are fasting and praying for the breakdown of Christian marriages and, in particular, the marriages of those in Christian leadership. But we need not be daunted by these threats. Satan, unlike God, is not present everywhere at the same time. And although he seems to have an efficient, well-tried network of evil with which he oppresses us, we must never forget that he is the defeated foe. As Christians we hold the trump card: prayer in the name of Jesus. The thrilling thing is that couples who obey the biblical injunctions and combat Satan and his minions by resisting him, fighting him and holding their ground (see Eph 6:13) are among those who are finding that, mysteriously and miraculously, their marriages are being mended by God. They are find that this spiritual solidarity against the powers of darkness works; in truth, that prayer still works.

CHAPTER 7
SEX: WHERE GOD DELIGHTS TO DO MIRACLES

WHEN A MAN AND WOMAN MARRY, GOD GIVES THEM A WEDDING present. He designed this gift himself. His intention was that his gift should bring lifelong pleasure to the couple concerned, that it should contribute to that oneness which would alleviate their loneliness. That gift is sexual intercourse.

God noticed that, even in paradise, Adam was lonely. To resolve this problem, God created woman, man's counterpart and companion, with great care. When she was presented to her husband, this woman came to the relationship genitally equipped to complement him so that he could slot into her body and, like two pieces of a two-piece jigsaw puzzle, they could unite to become one whole.

God knew that this design possessed all the potential needed to unite these two people in an indefinable, inseparable, enjoyable and mysterious union. So he instructed them from the beginning to fuse their bodies, and he promised that in so doing they would become one flesh—that is, one person consisting of two equal but complementary parts.

The call to married couples to unite their bodies in this unique act of oneness comes consistently from God through one book of the Bible after another. It appears first in the book of Genesis. Just as God instructs married people to "leave," to "cleave," and to become one socially, spiritually and psychologically, so he exhorts them to make sure that a sexual oneness is created and maintained: "a man leaves his father and his mother and cleaves to his wife, and they become one flesh" (Gen 2:24 RSV).

In other words, leaving, cleaving, oneness and fleshness (sexuality) go together. They enhance and enrich and feed each other. A couple cannot separate other onenesses from sexual oneness. They belong together.

The Bible and Sex

The importance of this sexual oneness is underscored in the book of Deuteronomy where we read: "If a man has recently married, he must not be sent to war or have any other duty laid on him. For one year he is to be free to stay at home and bring happiness to the wife he has married" (Deut 24:5).

The word used in the Hebrew for *bringing happiness* to one's wife means literally "to know sexually," to discover what, in particular, brings her sexual satisfaction. God so desired that couples should find for themselves the physical pleasure that his wedding present afforded that he required that they should give themselves to this task wholeheartedly during the formative months of their marriage.

And God continues to urge, through the author of Proverbs, that couples abandon themselves to the enjoyment of his wedding present: "May your fountain be blessed, and may you rejoice in the wife of your youth. . . . May her breasts satisfy you always, may you ever be captivated by her love" (Prov 5:18-19).

The word *fountain* used here refers to the husband's genitalia and his ability to conceive new life. It includes his desire for sexual intimacy. The implication here is that the male should recognize sexual desire for what it is—a gift from God, and that he should enjoy his wife's body because God intended that at the heart of wholesome marriages should lie healthy, zestful, satisfying sex.

The author of the Song of Songs echoes this sentiment and embroiders it with the most extravagant language used anywhere in the Bible to describe the passionate sense of oneness and contentment made possible by God's gift of sex. Into the mouth of the bride, the poet puts these words:

Let him kiss me with the kisses of his mouth—for your love is more delightful than wine. . . . My lover is to me a sachet of myrrh resting between my breasts. He has taken me to the banquet hall, and his banner over me is love. Strengthen me . . . for I am faint with love. His left arm is under my head, and his right arm embraces me (Song 1:2, 13; 2:4-6).

The Rewards of Satisfying Sex

The claim has been made that when sex is right, everything is right. Certainly it is true to say that sex colors every other aspect of the relationship: the social, the spiritual, the psychological. So when Jesus was questioned on the subject of marriage and divorce, he reiterated his Father's instructions and added to them: " 'A man will leave his father and mother and be united to his wife, and the two will become one flesh.' *So they are no longer two, but one"* (Mt 19:4-5, emphasis mine).

Paul builds on these scriptural foundations by warning couples that if they rob one another of the opportunity of the pure pleasure of sexual intimacy, they are giving Satan a foothold in their relationship. Since husband and wife are both vulnerable, this might lead to disaster. Speaking of sexual intercourse he writes: "A man should fulfil his duty as a husband, and a woman should fulfil her duty as a wife, and each should satisfy the other's needs. . . . Do not deny yourselves to each other, unless you first agree to do so for a while in order to spend your time in prayer; but then resume normal marital relations" (1 Cor 7:3-5 TEV). By normal marital relations Paul means regular, mutually satisfying sex—physical intimacy which communicates to both partners that they are uniquely loved.

Some Hidden Messages of Good Sex

The reason why God places such a heavy emphasis on sexual oneness is that sexual lovemaking is a profound nonverbal language. Both partners in marriage can learn this language. And both can use it to communicate to the other far more dimensions of intimacy than the language of words is capable of transmitting. Among other things, this "body language" says:

☐ You matter to me. I want to give myself supremely and completely and uniquely to you. My life is bound up in yours.

☐ I am committed to you wholeheartedly until death parts us.

☐ I appreciate you.

☐ You are precious to me—more precious than anyone else in the world.

☐ Thank you for who you are; for staying alongside me.

☐ I hope we shall be together as companions and lovers for many more years. I want to continue to venture into life with you.

☐ I find delight in your body, your sexuality. I love you in your God-given, God-created sexuality.

☐ My own body finds fulfilment in fusing itself with yours.

☐ I want our love to last forever. It will transcend the sorrows of life and be strengthened by its joys.

☐ I want nothing to come between us: no person, no attitude, no quarrel, no bitterness or sourness. I am all for you; I am on your side.

☐ I want to be one of God's instruments of healing, first and foremost to you.

In other words, God's wedding present to married couples, sexual intercourse, was intended to be a special meeting point in marriage where husband and wife could come together with such pleasurable closeness that new life would spring from every act of intercourse. This new life would not necessarily be in the form of babies, but rather in the form of a renewal of the couple's spiritual or social oneness, a deepening of their understanding of one another or a healing of some of the hurts which are inflicted on each of us as we walk through life.

Countless couples, however, have never even begun to enjoy the richness of sexual oneness. Sex, for them, is not a healing experience but a hurting one. Sex might even be one of the major causes contributing to the breakdown of their marriage. Several such couples known to me have discovered the truth of the title of this chapter: that sex is the place in marriage where God delights to perform miracles and that with this miracle comes another, the healing of their marriage.

Simon and Jane's Story

I first witnessed God perform this miracle many years ago. My husband and I were speaking at a conference for married people. I had given a

talk which outlined God's pattern for marriage and during the coffee
break a young man asked if he could talk to me. His name was Simon.
Simon told me that he would give anything to enjoy the kind of
relationship I had described. "We've got a lovely house," he said. "It's
full of the antiques which we've collected and which we're proud of.
We've got two cars. The kitchen is full of expensive gadgets. We've got
a beautiful garden—everything we want. And I'd exchange it all today
in return for good, satisfying sex—the kind of relationship you've been
talking about this morning. In fact, I'm not sure how much longer I
can carry on in our marriage unless things change."

I arranged to meet Simon later that day. His wife, Jane, and my
husband would come too. When we met as a foursome, I asked Simon
when sex became a problem instead of a pleasure. He looked puzzled
and thought aloud.

"Before we were married, it used to be fantastic," he admitted. "But
as soon as our two children were born, Jane lost interest. I remember
how she used to turn her back on me in bed. Then she made it clear
she didn't want me to touch her anymore. She even said she didn't like
kissing."

Jane burst in at this point: "It may have been fantastic for you before
we were married, but it wasn't fantastic for me. It was all so furtive.
I felt cheated and soiled. It ruined sex forever for me. I felt so guilty.
And if you want to know, I still feel guilty. I wish we'd never slept
together before we were married. I knew it was wrong at the time. But
you wanted it, so I gave in to you."

Simon had never heard Jane voice these guilt feelings before. He had
not realized that she thought sex outside of marriage was wrong. Neither of them were Christians at the time of their engagement, and it
never occurred to him to question whether premarital sex would upset
Jane in any way. Now, too late, he discovered the truth. The future

looked bleak.

When guilt holds a person in its grip, they can feel powerless. A kind of emotional paralysis creeps over them. For Jane, emotional and sexual paralysis had resulted in long-lasting sexual coldness toward Simon which she seemed unable to control.

But Jesus died on the cross of Calvary to pay the price for our sin. Therefore, no Christian need be bound by the kind of guilt which Jane described. David and I had the joy of explaining to Jane that though God's Word does make it clear that sexual intercourse has one context and one context only—marriage—even so, when people have fallen short of that standard, God does not condemn them to a life of misery and frigidity afterwards. He extends to them his undeserved, unearned, forgiving love.

For Jane this was news—such good news that she could scarcely drink it in. We went on to explain that if she confessed this sin to God, he would set her free from the guilt and from its power. He would set her free to express love to Simon in a physical way once more. We invited her to take the risk and to make that confession.

Although Simon and Jane were not used to praying aloud, they both told God how sorry they were that they had snatched sexual intimacy out of its God-given context, the marriage relationship. They asked him to forgive them.

Ours was the privilege of praying that God would apply the blood of Jesus to the sin and to the guilt and set Jane and Simon free from the consequences. We prayed that God would restore to them the delights of physical lovemaking which he had always intended them to enjoy. Nothing dramatic happened that day. Neither Simon nor Jane felt as though anything at all had happened. The conference ended.

Some months later, we received a message from them. God, they said, was answering that prayer and restoring to them, not just a sexual oneness which was animating their entire relationship, but a spiritual oneness such as they had never enjoyed before.

Henry and Brenda's Story

A similar miracle transformed Henry and Brenda's marriage. Although they attended a series of Marriage Fulfilment seminars, we did not speak to them personally. But two months after the seminars, we received a letter from Brenda in which she told us how God had mended their marriage.

They had been married for thirty-five years when they attended the seminars, but they had never known closeness of any kind. Twelve years earlier, Henry had undergone surgery, and while he was in the hospital he had suffered lung failure. Drugs were prescribed, and Henry believed that one of the side effects was that they had left him impotent. Consequently he refused even to try to make love to his wife. He had a little dog which he adored. The dog slept with Henry, and Brenda slept apart from them. "I was like a piece of the furniture to him, or so I felt," she admitted. The barriers between them widened.

Brenda became friendly with a younger man. After awhile they had an affair. But when she joined the local church, God convicted her of the sin in which she was involved and she learned there that if she would repent and give up seeing this young man, she would find what she was seeking—the way to God. She confessed the affair to God. She knew that God had forgiven her, and her joy was inexpressible when Henry joined the church too. Three months before the Marriage Fulfilment Weekend they were baptized together. But Brenda had not plucked up courage to tell Henry that she had deceived him. Depression had set in, and their marriage was shaky when they arrived to participate in the seminars.

God used the seminars to challenge both of them and to show them that he could restore crumbling marriages. They talked and talked. Brenda confessed. Henry forgave her. And Brenda forgave Henry. And suddenly a whole new future seemed to stretch before them. As Brenda put it: "We realized all we had been doing wrong and all we could achieve in the future, with God's help."

One of the first areas of their marriage which God restored was the sexual side. As Brenda expressed it in her letter: "We are as one at last and have experienced sexual fulfillment the last six weeks like we never thought possible again. The joy of our union and the many miracles recently are only a small part of the joy and wonder of our life."

Graham and Margaret's Story Continued

God performed a miracle of a rather different kind for Graham and Margaret, whom I mentioned in chapter five. You'll recall that Graham and Margaret longed for a baby. For seven years they waited. For seven years nothing happened. Sexual tensions and the emotional upsets I described earlier spoiled their physical lovemaking. Then, through the ministry of inner healing, God healed the hurts which had been inflicted on Margaret during her childhood, and she relaxed noticeably. She and Graham were growing in their understanding and love of one another. But they were unprepared for God's next move.

Within a week of this healing touch from God which was bringing about a radical change in Margaret's attitude to herself, to their marriage and to life in general, she conceived. They did not realize this at first, of course.

When they eventually discovered that Margaret was pregnant, they were filled with a feeling which Graham describes as "almost unbelief." "It took us a few weeks for it to sink in," Graham recalls. And Margaret recollects:

I was really bowled over because the ministry I had received was not specifically to ask God for a baby. It was to put right the past—and yet he answered in that wonderful way. And after all the years of thinking that God was just letting time drift by, it was astounding that he didn't waste any time at all when it really came to it and that really thrilled me.

When the news sunk in at last, it seemed as though a new day had dawned. It brought to them feelings of "extreme joy, a celebration and grateful thanks to God." And it transformed their sex life. They experienced what Graham describes as an "emptying of the fear" of years; a wonderful release. "Because the fear of the menstrual cycle had gone, we were able to enjoy each other so much more. And because the tension was gone, there was peace within which added to our enjoyment of one another physically."

As I listened to the tape on which Graham and Margaret recorded their memories and feelings, I listened, too, to the background noises—baby noises. Their five-month-old baby was grunting and cooing and making sucking sounds while her parents were talking to me. She was a tangible reminder that, with God, nothing is impossible—that sex is the place where he delights to do miracles.

Sex Phobia

Couples suffering from sex phobia, the fear of having intercourse, might wonder whether God's miracle-working power can reach their relationship. There was an occasion in my own marriage when God demonstrated to me that even this condition does not lie outside his miracle-working power or concern.

I used to love playing badminton. Each Friday afternoon would see me on the courts—until the day when I slipped a disc. My back was painful for several months, so David and I refrained from physical lovemaking lest it should intensify the pain.

At the end of a holiday in Greece, I remember running along the beach with my son and commenting to my husband that I thought my back was better. Two hours later, while driving through Yugoslavia, the camper in which we were traveling hit a tree and overturned, somersaulting down a fourteen-foot embankment. Blood trickled down my face. And as I lay on the grass beside the wrecked vehicle, I became conscious of a pain stabbing me between my shoulder blades. My back was injured in another place.

By the time this injury healed, we were accustomed to the life of celibacy. And when we realized that there was no longer a need for us to abstain from sexual intimacy, I recognized that I was too frightened to take the risk of abandoning my body to David. Supposing we did make love. What would it do to my back? Supposing my back was injured all over again! The fear was irrational, I knew. Phobias always are. But I seemed powerless to snap out of its clutches.

During the weekend for married couples which I have mentioned already in an earlier chapter (the occasion where God moved in and began the long process of mending our marriage), we listened to a talk on the joys of making love. After the talk, we spent nearly two hours comparing our own experience of sex with God's desire for us. We knew we wanted to change, but we did not know how this change could take place.

That evening, the leaders of the conference who were staying in our home asked us if we were enjoying the weekend. To my surprise, for we were not accustomed to sharing such intimacies with anyone in those days, the story of our sexual dysfunction tumbled out. Even as I heard my lips trace the demise of our sexual togetherness, I wished they would stop. I felt uncomfortable and feared that everyone else in the room would feel the same. It was also very late and I feared that we were being selfish in burdening other people with our woes when another busy day had yet to be faced.

But our friends seemed neither embarrassed about the problem we shared, nor concerned about the lateness of the hour. The only thing they expressed was concern for our relationship and that God should be brought into the situation. God? I had never thought of *praying* about this particular problem. But that is what these friends suggested, and that is what they did.

I remember how the four of them gathered around David and me. Quietly and gently, they laid hands on us and simply asked God to remove the fear which held me captive and to give to David a gentleness and sensitivity which would woo me back into enjoying God's wedding present once more.

There were no tongues of fire to reveal the presence of God. And there were no warm feelings which might suggest that the Spirit of God had been active inside me. We would have to wait to test for ourselves whether God had heard that prayer and whether he would answer it.

But we were not kept waiting long. Just as sunshine in spring warms even frostbitten buds, restores them and causes them to burst with new life, so God's healing love, released through this ministry of prayer with the laying on of hands, warmed me, drove away my fear and set me free to respond to my husband once more. And as God sensitized us to one another sexually that weekend, we were aware that he was mending many areas of our marriage at the same time.

Miracles in Slow Motion for Gary and Karen

I do not want to give the impression that when God performs a miracle in a marriage it is always painless and easy. Sometimes the miracle takes place slowly. Indeed, if the persons concerned were able to watch the miracle in slow motion and in retrospect, they would recognize that part of the miracle was that God gave them the grace to endure the pain through which they had to work before even the scent of a marriage-mending miracle could be detected. This was Karen and Gary's experience.

Gary, a full-time worker with Campus Crusade for Christ, was a "workaholic in his witnessing." He was out to save the world for Christ. When the first baby arrived, Karen tried to sacrifice her husband for the ministry, but, stuck at home all day with the baby, she grew increasingly lonely. From time to time Karen would plead with Gary to give quality time to her and the children, but each time the answer would be the same: he was too busy. And they had no money for vacations. In her loneliness, Karen's need for an intimate friend increased. When Gary began to pastor a church, his workload changed. But instead of recognizing the needs of his growing family, he poured himself out for the congregation and earned their praise by doing so.

The sexual side of their relationship deteriorated rapidly. After a long day alone with the children, looking after the home alone, and trying to help Gary with his secretarial work, Karen would be exhausted. Because of this fatigue, she would often fail to respond to Gary's advances. This made Gary bitter. He, too, had had a busy day but his desire for physical intimacy was not diminished. He interpreted Karen's lack of desire as rejection of him. And when Karen refused to join her body with his, he would punish her the next day by withholding the tenderness and kindness with which he treated her on the occasions when they did make love.

Because they were short of money, they decided to take a boarder. The boarder arrived and gave to Karen everything she had yearned for from her husband: "Our personalities seemed to fit together like two pieces of a jigsaw puzzle. Our conversation flowed effortlessly. He shared in depth with me about his childhood and what he loved. He listened intently to me as I shared my life story with him. He seemed to show so much interest in my ideas and thoughts."[21]

Consequently, Karen and the boarder, Dale (a married man working away from home), became infatuated with one another. Ignoring their marriage vows, they allowed their emotions to dictate their actions. As Karen expresses it: "I was completely captivated by him and felt compelled to ignore everything else in my life to concentrate totally upon him."[22]

When Gary discovered that Karen had been having an affair with Dale, he lost control of himself, attacked her physically and would have broken her neck if the elders of the church had not pulled him away from her just in time. Karen resolved to leave Gary. Any feelings she once had for him were dead; she was alive to Dale, so there seemed no point in returning.

But she did return. She confessed her sin to God. She and Gary recommitted themselves to one another and their relationship, and the miracle of marriage-mending began. But in her book *A Healing Season*, Karen shows that this miracle took them through pain before it relieved them of it:

Even though we were committed to each other, our healing was a very slow, long process. The hurt was strong and vivid. Everything around us seemed to remind us of our pain. One day while I was ironing, Gary walked into the room and saw a small slip of paper on the ironing board. The paper had a smile face on it. Gary broke down and cried because he knew I had always put smile faces on the cards I wrote to Dale. Gary would be struck by the intensity of his pain every time he . . . passed a motel where he knew Dale and I had stayed. Gary cried often, but I tried to comfort him and reassure him that I cared and that we *would* make it.

Yet words of reassurance were hard to say. I had lost all my love for Gary; my feelings had died. I was starting at ground level in rebuilding my relationship with him. My love for Dale had been so strong and romantic that it kept coming back to haunt me as I worked hard to build a love for Gary. Dale had been such an intimate part of my life that I couldn't seem to shake him from my thoughts. There was much to remind me of him, especially in my home where we had often been together."[23]

Gary and Karen prayed together and gave quality time to one another. Their church gave them two months leave so that they could concentrate on rebuilding their marriage. Even so, to attempt to return to physical lovemaking was hard for both of them. They were civil to one another, but no bond of affection held them together anymore. And just as Karen was plagued with thoughts of Dale and the love which still burned in her heart for him, so Gary was crushed in spirit, unable to control *his* thoughts: " 'Karen in the arms of another man! Will she ever love me as she had loved him? Will we ever be husband and wife again?' "[24]

But with God *anything* is possible. Gradually, slowly, almost imperceptibly at times, he turned the stagnant water of their marriage into the wine of a rich relationship. As Karen puts it: "Every area of marriage has changed. Sexually Gary and I have experienced a oneness and gratification that greatly surpasses love's betrayal."[25]

Gary and Karen, like the other couples I have mentioned in this chapter, have been changed. While they change, their relationships change, too, and the changes they enjoy have a touch of the miraculous about them. Karen expressed this change in a poem once:

Changed
Changed into lovers . . .
All it took was
death, rebirth,
and the touch

of a miraculous God.
Really, not much—
for God,
but confounding
for me.[26]

CHAPTER 8

FORGIVENESS BRINGS HEALING

THE MOST MOVING PRAYER RECORDED IN THE ENTIRE BIBLE IS the one Jesus cried from the cross: "Father, forgive them, for they do not know what they are doing" (Lk 23:34). When people come to God to receive this forgiveness for their many personal failures, they frequently find that, not only do their relationships with God change, but their marriages change also. At the foot of Christ's cross, they find the resources they need to nurse sick and ailing marriages.

This was certainly Pauline's experience. I wondered, at one stage, whether her marriage to Stephen could survive. Yet I have watched it grow not weaker, but stronger. When I invited Pauline to explain where the breakthrough in their relationship came from, her immediate reply was: "It all began with God."

Before Pauline became a Christian her marriage was finished so far as she was concerned. She had already left Stephen twice and had lost all motivation to work at a relationship which seemed to her totally lacking in the love she was searching for. But when she became a Christian, her attitude was turned inside out. Somehow she not only knew that she was responsible to recommit herself to work at this relationship, but she also knew God would give her the resources she needed to carry out that resolve.

At first Pauline expected God to do all the work of marriage mending for her and, attending a church which focused on God's healing power, she grew bitter and resentful that God refused to wave the magic wand which would solve all her marital problems immediately. But gradually she recognized that while God was withholding a dramatic, sensational healing, what he was offering was a slow, persistent and effective reconciliation between her and her husband. This would require cooperation from the two of them, and it would contribute to the maturing process of them both. She recognized that years of hard work lay ahead and that on the way she would probably fail many times. But the forgiveness of God which had motivated her to rework her relationship with her husband would always be available to her at the cross of Christ.

Pauline is still proving for herself the faithfulness of God in this situation as year by year she and Stephen grow closer to one another.

Commanded to Forgive

Jesus reminds us on many occasions that our responsibility is not simply to receive his free forgiveness for the failures which blight our lives. In addition to that, in all our relationships with other people, we have a responsibility to forgive anyone who has failed us in any way. So when Peter asks him the startling question: "Lord, how many times shall I forgive my brother when he sins against me? Up to seven times?" Jesus replies: "I tell you, not seven times, but seventy-seven times" (Mt 18:21-22). And Jesus goes further: "When you stand praying, if you hold anything against anyone, forgive him, so that your Father in heaven may forgive you your sins" (Mk 11:25).

Where married couples are taking this exhortation seriously and obeying this command of Jesus, they are finding that God is mending their marriages. Indeed, more marriages are completely mended through the grace of forgiveness than through any other method that I know of.

I think of a couple my husband and I met after one of our Marriage Fulfilment conferences where we had spoken on the need to forgive. This couple invited us to their home for a meal, because they were anxious to tell us their story.

They had not intended to come to the seminars which had been organized by their local church, but God seemed to insist that they should come, and so they gave away the concert tickets they had bought for that night and attended the meetings.

When they came, their marriage was in deep trouble. The husband was involved in full-time Christian work. His wife helped him as best she could, but she had the home to run and two small children to look after, so time was in short supply. On his own admission, the husband was a workaholic. It rarely occurred to him to spend time with the family or take his wife out. He was overtired, his wife was overtired, and whenever they were together quarrels would erupt.

Their children grew increasingly aware of the friction between their parents and consequently became frighteningly insecure. "They refused to sleep at night," the wife explained. "They would wake up crying, wanting to come into Mummy and Daddy's bed. They were frightened that we were going to separate; that if they went to sleep in their own beds, they would wake up in the morning and find that one of us had gone for good."

At the end of the seminar on forgiveness, we had given couples an opportunity to recall habits or attitudes in their partner which they disliked or which had caused them to be hurt or upset. Then we asked a question: "Will you forgive your partner for that?"

In the silence which followed, couples were invited to forgive their partners. Unknown to the other, as they knelt beside one another in the church, these two both forgave each other. When the meeting ended, tears were rolling down their cheeks as they asked one another that most healing of all questions: "Will you forgive me for the way I have failed you and our marriage?" As they responded to that question, they resolved to live differently in the days that lay ahead.

When they returned home, they tried to explain to their children what had happened and told them that Mummy and Daddy would not be quarrelling anymore in the way they had been doing for months. The children slept soundly. And while we were there, both children played outside quite happily, showing no signs of insecurity. For this family, forgiveness brought healing not simply to the marriage but to the entire family. "It was worth giving away those concert tickets," the husband said. "God had something much better in store for us than good music."

The Meaning of Forgiveness

To forgive, according to *The Shorter Oxford English Dictionary*, means, among other things, to cease to harbor resentment, to pardon an offender or an offence, to give up resentment against someone, to abandon one's claim against a debtor, to make excuse for someone who has hurt you, to regard them indulgently. In other words, it means to let the offender off the hook; to deal graciously with that person.

Neville Ward has described forgiveness in this way: "Forgiving is love managing to continue though injured or dismayed or mystified."[27] It is bearing injury without retaliation. It is the capacity to be hurt but to continue to love without that love becoming "even just a little frightened and therefore more cautious and reserved."[28] It is seeking to understand why the offender inflicted the hurt in the first place, and so identifying with the offender's need or sorrow or deprivation that love for him or her deepens and becomes more sensitive to him or her as a person.

Forgiveness holds nothing against the offender: no grudge, no resentment, no anger, no ill feeling. Forgiveness is the Christlike generosity which restores broken relationships. Forgiveness is undeserved love which may or may not be accompanied by warm feelings. Such forgiveness brings healing to the most battered of relationships.

But such forgiveness does not come easily to most of Christ's followers—as Henry discovered. I introduced Henry in the preceding chapter. During one of the Marriage Fulfilment conferences we led, he and his wife, Brenda, drew so close to one another that their sexual relationship was transformed beyond their wildest dreams. But Brenda had confessed the adulterous relationship she had indulged in with a younger man and, although Henry forgave her initially, he took back this forgiveness and replaced it with a desire for revenge "which lay like a stone on his heart for many months," alongside anger, bitterness resentment and ugly threats. Why should this person go free? Could such sin ever really be forgiven?

For months, Henry seemed to find satisfaction in fingering his wounds. He even convinced himself that he had a right to feel resentful.

In a sick kind of way, he enjoyed the victimization. Henry is not the buoyant extrovert who forgets injuries easily. Rather, he is an introvert, the sort of person who finds it much more difficult to let go of resentments and hurts. But Henry discovered, through pain and turmoil, that until he did let go, the growth of their marriage was stunted. Indeed, his own relationship with God was in jeopardy. Jesus puts this clearly and solemnly in the parable of the unforgiving servant.

Jesus' Teaching on Forgiveness

In Matthew 18:21-35, Jesus tells the story of a king who decided to check his servants' accounts. Finding that a particular servant owed him large sums of money, he summoned the servant and demanded repayment of the debt. The servant pleaded with his master. There was no way he could gain access to such a large sum of money. Whereupon the king released him, cancelling the huge debt.

A fellow servant owed this man a few dollars. On leaving the king's presence, with this generous act of forgiveness fresh in his mind, the servant sought out his fellow servant and demanded instant payment of the small sum this man owed. The fellow servant pleaded for patience and mercy. But the merciless servant responded by throwing him into prison until he could pay. When this news reached the king, he was angry and called the servant back: " 'You worthless slave!' he said. 'I forgave you the whole amount you owed me, just because you asked me to. You should have had mercy on your fellow servant, just as I had mercy on you' " (Mt 18:32-33 TEV).

Jesus is implying here that, when he died on Calvary's cross and prayed that heart-rending prayer, "Father, forgive them," what he was saying was: "Father help them. Let them go. Set them free from every single sin they have ever committed and every sin they will commit in the future. Deal generously with them. Because of my death, release them from sin's bondage." In comparison with the enormity of this generous gesture, what he requires of us—that we let off the hook anyone who offends or hurts us—is but a small request.

When this realization seeped slowly, gradually and painfully into Henry's awareness, he forgave Brenda again. And again, they were free to work at their love. It was not easy—but love does work for those who work at it. Brenda listed some of its benefits: "We pray together night and morning, and we read the Bible together. We share and talk together and although age wise we are no chickens(!), our love life has improved tremendously even though there are medical difficulties (such as being overweight, tiredness, arthritis and, recently, a virus infection). I realize how much Henry loves me, and I love him—which is what really matters."

Some Steps to Forgiveness

We must forgive as readily and generously as Jesus forgave us because until we do, we are imprisoned by the thing we hold on to. Nature illustrates this superbly. For example, near the cottage where I am staying, rhododendron bushes cling to the hillside, delighting us all with their flamboyant colors in early summer. But the roots of some of these bushes are doing untold damage. Over the years, they have entwined themselves around the pine trees which grow alongside them and consequently the pine trees are slowly being strangled. If the roots would let go of the pine trees, the rhododendron roots would be free to spread themselves below ground, to burrow deep into the rich soil and at the same time, release the pine trees to be the fine, upstanding trees they were always intended to be.

The same principle applies to our attitudes. When negative, poisonous emotions like bitterness, hatred, resentment, anger or jealousy grow in us, we become their captives. They weaken our resilience and sometimes bite into our bodies also in the form of ulcers and hernias, migraine and backache. And we are so consumed by these tangled feelings which cling to us that we are no longer free to receive from God the resources with which he wants to nourish us: love, joy, peace, wholeness.

But when, with an act of the will, we take the plunge and ask God to cut us free from these negative emotions, a miracle happens: the miracle of reconciliation. I sometimes think of it in this way. To forgive means "to let go," "to let someone off the hook." So, when someone has hurt or offended me and I am conscious of bitterness or resentment in my life, I imagine that I am holding these emotions in my hands, with my fists clenched around them. Then, with an act of the will, I uncurl my hand and imagine the negative feelings falling to the ground. Then I hold my open and cupped hands up to God and ask him to fill them with love and joy and peace.

When the offending person is my husband, as is often the case, I am free, he is free and our relationship is free. That is why, when we conduct Marriage Fulfilment retreats, David and I like to spell out some of the steps couples can take to ensure that their forgiveness of one another is both regular and complete, so that this experience of freedom and joy becomes theirs.

Step 1: Be honest. Recognize that within your heart lurks seeds of anger, bitterness, resentment, jealousy, revenge, unforgiveness. Tell God that these thoughts and feelings are present and strong.

Step 2: Make a choice. You can either choose to cling to these thoughts and feelings, or you can choose to let go of them. Choose to drop them. Unclench your fists. Let the poison go. Pray a prayer like the following:

Lord Jesus, you know how my wife hurt me yesterday, but because you require it of me and because our marriage matters more to me than hanging on to this hurt, with an act of the will I forgive her.

Father, you know how my husband upset me just now, you know how the anger burns in my heart. I hand that anger to you. Sift it. Hand back to me only the anger which is righteous. Throw the rest away. And now, with an act of my will, I choose to forgive my husband.

Step 3: Ask God to show you how he feels about your partner. Wait for an answer to your question.

Step 4: Ask God to forgive you for harboring bitterness and resentment, jealousy and anger. Ask him to lance the abscess and drain away all the poison which has collected inside you.

Step 5: Ask God to pour his love onto your partner; to enrich him or her.

Step 6: Ask God to implant some of that love in you so that you can go back into the relationship with fresh supplies of love to give to your spouse.

Step 7: Ask God to touch and soothe and heal any hurts inside you or your partner that came from the altercation.

Step 8: Ask God to change you so that your marriage can be improved.

Step 9: Ask God to show you whether there is something specific you can do to show that you long for reconciliation and not the perpetuation of conflict.

Step 10: Ask God to melt any remaining hardness in your heart so that you are free to return to the relationship with your attitude softened by the love of God.

Step 11: Ask your spouse a question: "Will you forgive me?"

Step 12: Make an apology: "I'm sorry"—even if you believe that you are innocent!

None of these steps is easy, but each of them brings us one step nearer to uttering the complete prayer of forgiveness which releases love—the love which mends marriages. I never cease to marvel at the reality of the reconciliation which takes place between two people who forgive one another genuinely.

One of the most beautiful examples I know of occurred at a Marriage Fulfilment retreat. During one session we emphasized that, just as the Bible exhorts couples to leave and to cleave, to become one socially, emotionally and spiritually and to fuse their bodies sexually, so it commands us to keep short accounts with one another: to forgive. I told the story of Tom, a Black child who lived in Alabama.

Tom used to deliver newspapers every day to White men during their afternoon naps. One day, he was doing his newspaper route as usual when he felt an urgent need to go to the toilet. Looking round, he could see there was no toilet in the vicinity except the one reserved for Whites. Tom knew the law of Alabama: Blacks are not permitted to enter premises belonging to Whites. But Tom was desperate. He looked up and down the road. There was no one in sight. He reasoned with himself that, since it was nap time, everyone would be resting. Placing his pile of newspapers on the pavement, he went into the toilets.

Tom had never been in such an elegant place before and so, having used the toilet, he stopped to look round at the posters on the wall and to feel the cool of the tiles under his toes. He was so absorbed with the surroundings that he failed to hear footsteps behind him. But suddenly, he became aware of a White man towering over him. The White man's face flushed with anger when he saw a Black boy polluting territory reserved for Whites. He seized Tom by the scruff of the neck and rubbed his face in his own urine before the terrified boy could escape by diving between the White man's legs.

Outside the toilet, Tom ran into the arms of a big Black man. By this time Tom was sobbing uncontrollably. Between his sobs, he blurted out his story. The man he told was Dr. Martin Luther King, Jr.

When he had heard the whole sad saga, Dr. King helped Tom to understand that he was now faced with a choice. Either he could go home, tell all his friends and neighbors and relatives what had happened and thus perpetuate the hatred which already existed between Blacks and Whites, or he could forgive the man. Then Dr. King challenged the boy: "Forgive him, Tom. You can't harbor hatred in your heart forever."

A profound silence filled the room as this story reached its climax, and I could tell that God was challenging several people. I noticed tears in the eyes of one woman in particular. When the session was over, this woman asked to see me. When we met later in my room, she told me her story.

Her first marriage had ended in divorce. She had been married to her second husband for two years and this relationship, too, was deteriorating. The initial euphoria had worn off. She was missing the independence she had enjoyed when she lived alone after her first marriage broke up. And she was frightened because she had discovered that her husband could be violent. He had, in fact, bruised her on several occasions, and she feared that this would become more frequent if the tensions between them were not resolved. As a result, she was full of bitterness, resentment and anger and fear. She poured out a long list of grievances against her husband. She was ready to leave him and go to live with one of her children from her first marriage.

But Tom's story and God's challenge through Dr. King—"forgive!"—had penetrated her hardness, piercing her heart like an arrow. And now she was struggling. Deep down she wanted to forgive; to work at the relationship so that it survived. Did I think she could bring herself to go through with this act of forgiveness? Her feelings for her husband were stone cold. Could the old warmth be restored?

There was a childlikeness about this woman that I liked. Although outwardly she was frightened, anxious and tense, I could tell that inwardly she was deeply committed to making her husband happy and to living life God's way.

I pointed out that true forgiveness involves not warm feelings, but the will. The issue at stake was not could she forgive but would she let go of the resentments? "So the question to ask yourself is not 'can I forgive?' but 'will I forgive?' " I suggested. She remained silent for several minutes. Suddenly, the anxious lines creasing her face vanished and were replaced with a plucky smile. "I will," she said with a note of determination in her voice. "But I hope I don't regret it tomorrow!"

I suggested that we should turn her resolve into prayer. Although she was quite unaccustomed to praying aloud, she insisted on kneeling with me on the floor of my room.

As we had talked, she had already gone through some of the steps of forgiveness, by recognizing the poison which had been collecting in her heart like little pockets of pus. She had also made her choice: to let go of the resentment and bitterness and anger. So I invited her to picture our Lord hanging on the cross and to imagine herself standing at the foot of that cross with her husband. "Look at the cross," I said. "Try to recall just how generous Jesus' forgiveness for you has been. Look from Jesus to your husband, and when you are ready, pray the prayer Jesus prayed: 'Father, forgive him, he didn't know what he was doing. Father, release him, pardon him, he didn't realize how much he was hurting me.' "

Again, there was a long silence while she summoned her resolve. Then, she echoed that prayer of Jesus and I had the privilege of praying for her that God, by his Spirit, would lance the abscess inside her and drain away all the bitterness and resentment and anger which had collected there. I also prayed that God would replace these negative emotions with a fresh and genuine love for her husband; that he would show her ways in which she could express that love. After we had finished praying, I suggested that the next day I might chat with the two of them if they felt I could help them renegotiate their relationship on a new set of terms.

Next morning, at breakfast, I noticed that they both looked ten years younger. Their faces radiated contentment, joy and bewildered wonder. After the meal they told me that while the wife had been with me, letting go of her bitterness, her husband had been praying with someone else, asking God to work similarly in him. When they met up together that night they had asked forgiveness of one another and experienced the unexpected but joyous reconciliation they were now enjoying. God had shown them what they needed to do to build on this newfound love, so there was no need for them to talk about their relationship anymore. God had rescued them from the pit.

Forgiving Yourself: Colin and Christine's Story

We've seen that God longs that we should replenish our own resources with his forgiveness so that we can, in turn, extend forgiving love to others. At the same time, he longs that we should apply that forgiveness to ourselves when we were at fault in the relationship.

Colin knew the theory: it was important to forgive himself. But he could not bring himself to do it, and so his wife persuaded him to come me to talk the problem over. Together they told me the trauma they had suffered.

Prior to coming to see me, Colin had been having an affair with his wife's closest friend. He had kept up the deceit for several months but eventually his wife, Christine, had found out and he had confessed. Christine was hurt, of course, but she believed in their marriage and was quick to blame herself. She could see where her friend had given Colin a quality of love which she had denied him. Now she wanted to use this crisis to build up their relationship, not to allow circumstances to tear it down. So as soon as Colin repented, she forgave him.

"But the problem is," Colin blurted out, "I just can't forgive myself. I feel so unworthy of Chris's love after what I've done."

I asked Colin whether he knew how God felt about him. He explained that this was a question he dared not ask himself. He loved the Lord, but his own unfaithfulness had destroyed all confidence in himself.

I went on to suggest that he, too, should try to picture Jesus hanging on the cross and that he should ask the Lord a direct question: "Lord, you know what I've done. Will you forgive me?" He agreed to do this, so we started to pray together.

It was not long before Colin could see, with his imagination, the form of Jesus dangling from the cross, so he asked the question I had suggested. The answer came straight back: "Of course, I forgive you. It was for this purpose that I died." Tears rolled down Colin's face: tears of gratitude, relief and wonder that a holy God would let him off the hook even after he had committed such a gross sexual sin.

"Jesus has forgiven you," I said after a long pause. "Will you now join sides with him and let yourself off the hook?" Colin told me afterwards that at first the question brought to the surface all the self-loathing and self-despising he had struggled with ever since his sin had been discovered. "I felt like a leper, scourged with my own sin," he admitted. But gradually, he realized that until he refused to let go of this self-hatred, he was, in fact, fighting against God rather than cooperating with him in refusing to agree with him.

He asked God to give him further confirmation that he was forgiven. This time, into his mind came a picture of Jesus with the woman caught committing adultery. He knew that he had stood in that same place of condemnation. But this time he heard Jesus say: "What you have done is wrong, but I do not condemn you. Go back and sin no more. Rather, pour into your relationship the love you were pouring elsewhere."

When Colin explained to Christine and me what was happening, he wept, Christine wept and tears trickled down my face too. It was a wonderfully healing moment to watch these two locked in a prolonged, warm and reconciling embrace.

With his arm still around Chris's shoulders, Colin told us the rest of the story. "When Jesus told me he didn't condemn me, I couldn't hang on to all that hatred of myself. He'd forgiven me, so the least I could do was to forgive myself. So I dropped the anger—just let it go. Then I felt this peace spread right through me. It started with my head, then spread through my mind, down through my chest, through to my emotions and it held me. Suddenly I knew I was free: free from the guilt, free from the sin, free from the past and free to love Chris and the kids again."

John Powell once wrote: "The acknowledged need for forgiveness is the most effective means of restoration for wounded spirits. No relationship should go on for very long without it."[29] As Chris and Colin left me that day, I recognized afresh how true those words are and gave silent thanks to God that once again the grace of forgiveness had given birth to another miracle: the healing which would result in a mended marriage.

CHAPTER 9

SAVED BY SUBMITTING

A CARD STANDING ON MY DESK BEARS THIS MESSAGE: "THERE ARE some defeats more triumphant than victories." Next to it stands a quotation from one of John Powell's books:

Every relationship must have crises. They are really invitations to rise above those soft plateaus where we want to linger permanently. Crises are definitely invitations to growth, and those who courageously accept these invitations will find a new and fresh dimension in their love-relationship.[30]

I first suspected that Dave and Gill were responding to this invitation to grow when they scribbled a note on the bottom of the Christmas card they sent one year. In two sentences, they thanked my husband and me for the help we had tried to give them and hinted that God was at work mending their marriage. Intrigued, I invited them to tell me what had been happening.

Dave and Gill had enjoyed a wonderfully carefree relationship when they first met in the youth group at their church, but when Gill went to college all that changed. Unable to see one another every day, they pined for each other and when they did meet, one weekend in three, they spent most of the weekend dreading the impending separation.

When Dave finished his studies, he moved to the town where Gill was a student and, though they were delighted to see one another regularly again, this very proximity presented them with a new set of problems. One was an accommodation crisis. Dave lived in a small studio apartment and Gill lived in the YWCA. When that closed down, she was homeless. The only available accommodation, it seemed, was another studio apartment in the same house as Dave's.

Having been apart for so long, their relationship had grown increasingly intense sexually, and now, with no restrictions placed on them, they succumbed to temptation and started to sleep together. They were both Christians. They knew that this activity was wrong. But they seemed unable to break out of the pattern once they had established it. This created an inevitable gulf between themselves and God which seemed unbridgeable. As Gill explained it to me: "We felt we couldn't go to God with the problem because we thought he wouldn't love us anymore." Far from God, the one who had brought them together in the first place, guilt pushed them further from one another as well.

The Love of God
Nevertheless, Dave asked Gill to marry him, and she said a ready yes. Their engagement was a stormy one during which problems seemed to

bombard them with alarming regularity and ferocity. Dave found it impossible to find a job, for one thing. Their car kept breaking down, for another. And money was always in short supply. Because the rift between themselves and God was widening, neither of them had the necessary spiritual resources to draw on to help them ride these storms, and so constant arguments would erupt.

By the time they married, Dave had found a job. With the job came a company car. Gill's father gave them a gift which enabled them to buy a house, and they imagined that, surrounded by comparative comfort, they would settle down to live happily together. They soon realized that their material possessions could not provide them with the marital joy they were searching for, and their relationship fell into a further state of disrepair. As Dave remembers it: "We wouldn't share, wouldn't communicate, wouldn't be intimate. We were two people living in the same house but not really living as a married couple."

And as Gill added: "Or we went the other way and fought all the time. We used to have terrible fights through anger and frustration."

One reason for their coldness toward each other was sexual dysfunction. Their lovemaking had failed to satisfy them before they were married, but they put that down to guilt. When, after they were married, they still failed to satisfy one another, they felt bitter. At first, they decided that since neither of them seemed capable of giving sexual pleasure to the other, they would just live with the problem and not have sexual intercourse. Then they decided to seek help from a sex therapist through the Marriage Guidance Council. But Gill disliked the therapist, objected to speaking to any man besides Dave about the intimacies of lovemaking and felt that Dave should somehow "just know" how to be the perfect, experienced lover who could satisfy her sexually. After all, she had bought him several sex manuals so that he could learn! When the therapist so much as hinted that she might have a part to play in ensuring that she and Dave enjoyed mutually satisfying sex, she accused him of "always picking on" her. Halfway through the course, she refused to attend any more sessions.

When Gill opted out of the sex therapy, Dave despaired of her and of their relationship. Sometimes he resigned himself to a marriage without sex. At other times he threatened to leave Gill (though he admits that he probably would not have acted out this threat). Life was bearable only because he busied himself outside the home. In the home, unhappiness and disillusionment took root, and Gill and Dave held out little hope that their marriage would ever improve.

At this stage of their lives a girl at work, Denise, befriended Gill. The genuineness and transparency of Denise's life had stood out to Gill for some months. This gave Gill the confidence to unburden herself to Denise, and Gill was to be further amazed by the depth of commitment to prayer and care that Denise showed her and Dave at this time.

When the bridges between them were firmly established, Denise invited Dave and Gill to go along to her church with her. They agreed. The first thing that struck them was the sense of the presence of God in the services. And the second was the obvious power of prayer. They witnessed for themselves how God touched and healed a girl suffering from anorexia nervosa and saw him make provision for several people who had been laid off.

The power this prayer generated stirred up in both of them a fresh thirst for God. They joined a home-fellowship group attached to the church and were overwhelmed by a third thing: the depth of understanding and love showered on them by the people in the group. They recalled that it was at this time that Dave lost his job. They had no funds with which to pay off a pile of bills. A member of this group anonymously dropped an envelope through the mail shoot in their door one night. The envelope contained a large sum of money and a note assuring them of prayer support.

This kind of support melted their hearts and persuaded them to put right their relationship with God. As Gill recalls the sequence of events: "We decided that we wouldn't concentrate on all our sexual problems; we'd get to know the Lord again and start from scratch, as it were."

They each made a definite act of recommitment to God. As an outward sign of this inward commitment, they decided to be baptized together.

Before the service they both embarked on a period of heart searching. For Gill these were weeks of deep and real repentance when she turned her back on many of the attitudes and patterns of the past and asked God's forgiveness for specific sins. Unlike Gill, Dave did not agonize over the past or search his heart to unearth specific sins. He simply handed the whole dismal picture to God and, in a matter-of-fact, businesslike way confessed, "I'm a sinner. I want you, Lord, to take the reins of my life from now on."

A New Start with God

Gill tried to recapture how spiritually intoxicated she felt as she emerged from the baptistry knowing that God had washed them both clean:

> I felt a real joy and release and an inflowing of the Holy Spirit. It was lovely. I really felt that physically—as if I was being filled from the toes all the way up—felt a sort of warmth spreading up my body. But I realize it's not a question of *feeling* I was forgiven but *knowing* I was forgiven as much as anything. I know the Lord doesn't hold anything against me so there's no need to hold anything against myself. I left my burdens at the foot of the cross. And I walked away without them because that's what Jesus died for.

Dave, too, was touched by God during that service, and I could see for

myself that a radical change had taken place not only in their relationship with God but also with each other. Remembering how tense, angry
and bitter they used to be, and witnessing for myself how tender and
affectionate and caring they now were toward one another, I marveled
aloud: "It's as though God has given you a completely new start. In
fact, it seems as though your marriage is just beginning. But what, in
particular, made the difference?"

Gill reached for her Bible and explained that since they had reded-
icated their lives to God, they had begun to use God's Word, the Bible,
as a manual—"Just like you have a car manual, we have a marriage
manual," she said. They had been looking up references to marriage
in this manual and had stumbled across all kinds of instructions which
had previously escaped them. "For instance, I found this one." Gill
read from Paul's letter to the Ephesians:

> Wives, submit to your husbands as to the Lord. For the husband
> is the head of the wife as Christ is the head of the church, his body,
> of which he is the Savior. Now as the church submits to Christ, so
> also wives should submit to their husbands in everything. (Eph
> 5:22-24)

"When I read those verses I felt that I should be a submissive wife to
Dave and follow his instructions and decisions instead of fighting with
him and always wanting what I wanted," Gill went on. "I was a very
selfish sort of person, making so many demands on Dave, not consid-
ering him at all. So I learned, and am still learning, to be submissive
to Dave and to let him take the lead and to set the direction—a spiritual
direction, physical direction and emotional direction—following his
hopes and plans and desires."

I knew Gill well enough to recognize that the Holy Spirit who had
filled her with the love of Jesus at her baptism was continuing to effect
real and rapid changes in her life, transforming her into the likeness of

the God she now followed. She went on to explain to me how this transformation was taking place. When reading her Bible one day, she came across some more verses on the marriage relationship in Peter's first epistle. This verse, in particular, challenged her: 'Your beauty should not come from outward adornment. . . . Instead, it should be that of your inner self, the unfading beauty of a gentle and quiet spirit, which is of great worth in God's sight" (1 Pet 3:3-4).

"I realized when I read that verse that I didn't have that at all—a gentle and quiet spirit. So I began to pray for it and it's made a big difference."

Immediate Changes

As they continued to chat with me, I detected for myself three immediate and major differences in their relationship. The first was that, because Gill was now supportive rather than manipulative, they were becoming increasingly skilled at handling conflict creatively. Gill admitted that before she bumped into this life-changing verse and the concept of submission, she placed no trust at all in Dave's judgment:

I didn't trust Dave at all. In fact, I thought that he'd made such a mess of everything in the past—*he* was the one who had got us into all the troubles—that if I just trusted myself and got my own way perhaps things would work out better. Even if he had good ideas, I felt they wouldn't work, so I talked him out of them.

Dave added:

The real difference is that Gill used to make her own mind up about a situation and refuse to accept anything I would say or any leadership from me, because she thought I was a right idiot. She used to literally shout me down and I'd give in—anything for a quiet life. I'd never had anybody shout at me in my upbringing at home, and I didn't know how to deal with the situation.

When Gill made her commitment to submit, all that changed. She laughed as she observed: "It's much easier to resolve problems if you're not going to shout at each other over them, if you're going to talk them over and be sensitive to the way each other feels and cares. We don't panic in the same way that we used to about our crises. We talk them over and pray about them and resolve them in that way. And we're much happier."

Since Gill stopped blackmailing Dave emotionally, cornering him so that he gave her her own way in everything, the sexual problems which had caused them so much heartache from the start are beginning to right themselves. The key to this problem, too, Gill believes, is submission. Whereas she used to demand that Dave should take all the initiative and ensure that every wish and whim of hers was attended to, now she recognizes that in this most intimate part of their relationship she must give as well as receive. Her first concern must be to bring pleasure to Dave and not to demand that he should bring pleasure to her. "It's funny," she recalled. "When my attitude changed and I concentrated on making Dave happy, I relaxed and found that I was having a whale of a time. I really enjoyed myself."

Gill prayed that she might take this word *submission* seriously. She started affirming Dave for the things he does well rather than constantly blaming him for the things he fails to do. She started thinking positively and constructively and creatively about their relationship instead of making a whole string of selfish demands. Since then, she has found that she is no longer defeated by marriage but thoroughly committed to it. She was the first to admit that they have a long way to go before they can claim that truly their marriage has been mended. "But then," she smiled, "we're married for life aren't we? If we don't get things right tomorrow, we've got plenty more years to work at putting them right."

Some Meanings of Submission

After Dave and Gill left me, I turned the word *submission* over and over in my mind. For Dave and Gill it had been the master key that unlocked so many doors. But what does it really mean? Does it mean that Gill has to become Dave's doormat, kowtowing to every suggestion he makes? I looked back at that chapter in Ephesians which Gill had read, and I noticed that Paul says this: "Wives, submit to your husbands as to the Lord. For the husband is the head of the wife as Christ is the head of the church, his body, of which he is the Savior" (Eph 5:22-23). I compared it with 1 Corinthians 11:3: "Now I want you to realize that the head of every man is Christ, and the head of the woman is man, and the head of Christ is God."

The word Paul selects for *head* is the same word we in the West in the twentieth century use when we describe that part of our body which houses the brain and the eyes and the ears: the seat of decision-making, discernment and acquired and inspired wisdom; the place where thoughts are sifted, refined choices made, plans instigated; the place from which guidance is given to the rest of the body.

But as John Stott points out so helpfully in his book *Issues Facing Christians Today* (Marshalls, 1984), Paul, the first-century theologian, knew nothing of neuroscience. When Paul used the word *head* to describe the husband's role, therefore, he was not giving the husband a carte blanche for making all the family decisions, nor was he giving him the right to bulldoze such decisions through. No, what Paul is implying is that headship has nothing to do with rights to be enjoyed. Rather the husband's headship involves a series of responsibilities to be performed.

For just as Jesus, the head of the church, takes upon himself the responsibility of protecting and nourishing and cherishing his bride, the church, so the husband must pattern his style of loving on that of

Jesus and, in turn, protect and nourish and cherish his wife, and in this way become God's instrument of healing for her. This is what headship involves. This is what every woman needs, whether she recognizes it or not. But no man can exercise this kind of headship unless his wife is prepared to cooperate: to be protected, nourished and helped by her husband.

Submission Sets Us Free

My mind went back to the days when God was mending and revitalizing our own marriage and I realized that, just as God had used this one word *submission* to cause Gill to do a U-turn in her thinking and relating to her husband, so he had challenged me with that same word.

I was not manipulative. I didn't shout down my husband's ideas, brainwashing him into accepting that I was right. My problem was the complete opposite. When I married David I was shy, inarticulate and immature. He was strong, and I welcomed his strength and decisiveness. The spiritual strength which was the result of his close walk with God in student days was what attracted me to him in the first place. He was, I suppose, rather like a protective father-figure under whose shadow I delighted to relax and who rescued me from the need to think things through for myself.

In student days this meant that if I had a problem with my theological studies, I would go to him for advice. After we were married, if he asked me, "What shall we do on our day off this week?" or "What color shall we decorate the spare bedroom?" I would reply, "I really don't mind. You decide." He did decide. And I did not mind. I respected him and enjoyed being led by him. What is more, I thought I was being a thoroughly submissive wife.

But the work of God's Spirit is to change us, to stretch us, to free us to become the strong, capable people he always intended that we should be. Because David's love for me drew out my potential as a person and because the Holy Spirit worked deeply in my life over the years, I ceased to be the mouselike character David had married and grew instead into a full-fledged person. And then our problems began! I discovered that I had a mind of my own. I also began to voice my likes and dislikes. Instead of leaving the decision-making entirely to David, I would express my opinions, sometimes questioning David's wisdom and judgment.

He, in turn, both valued and resented the changes that he saw taking place in me. On the one hand he welcomed a wife who sharpened his own thinking, but on the other hand he pined for the sweet, unquestioning "yes-wife" who had rubber-stamped every suggestion he had made. And I was caught between these two equally powerful emotions. He used to tell me that I was "a very powerful woman." Sometimes he would say this approvingly, at other times despairingly. I grew increasingly frustrated as sometimes he encouraged me to express my newfound strengths, and at other times he seemed to squash them. And I hated the label *powerful woman*. I could not see that womanly strength and wifely submission could possibly fit hand in glove.

One day, while I was making a special study of Christian marriage for a book I was writing on the subject, and while I was immersed in material for the chapter on headship and submission, I turned to the same chapter of Ephesians God used to speak to Gill, and I focused my attention on one phrase: "Wives, submit to your husbands *as to the Lord*" (Eph 5:22, emphasis mine).

" 'As to the Lord.' That's the key," I said to myself. "But what does it mean?" I thought back to the day I turned to Christ. I was sitting in a meeting where an evangelist spelled out, simply and forthrightly, the extent of the love that burns in God's heart for us. At the end of the meeting, he invited people to make a personal response to that love.

I did. From that moment on, Isaac Watts' lovely hymn, "When I Survey the Wondrous Cross" summed up the guiding principles of my life:

Were the whole realm of Nature mine,
That were an offering far too small;
Love so amazing, so divine,
Demands my soul, my life, my all!

Or, as I like to sing in place of that last line, "*shall have* my soul, my life, my all."

"When I submitted my life to the Lord," I thought to myself, "I surrendered to him everything I had and everything I am. That's submission."

I thought of women in the Bible and began to tease out what submission to Jesus meant for them. In particular, I concentrated on Mary, the mother of Jesus. David and I had visited Nazareth on one occasion and had seen the church which has been built over the spot where the angel Gabriel is supposed to have appeared to Mary when he announced that she was to be the mother of the Messiah. I had knelt in that church and tried to identify with the enormity of the "yes" Mary gave to God that day. And I had realized that what she was saying, in effect, was: "Here I am, Lord, totally available to you. Take my body, my emotions, my sexuality, my time, my material possessions such as they are. Take all of my resources. Everything I have and everything I am is placed at your disposal. Do with me what you will. I am yours."

On a subsequent visit to Israel, I measured the distance between Galilee, where Jesus lived and worked and ministered, and Jerusalem, where Jesus spent the last week of his life. I realized that it would have taken Jesus and his followers days to walk from Capernaum via Jericho to Jerusalem. What is more, the going must have been tough. The sun would have scorched them during the day. The ground would have been uneven and rough. And the road running from Jericho to Jerusalem was notoriously dangerous. Yet we read that the women from Galilee stayed with him right up to the crucifixion and beyond. Their devotion to him was such that they were prepared to sacrifice time and talents, comfort and convenience, money and possessions for this man who had captured their hearts.

Then I turned to the Old Testament where I found the same basic principle staring me in the face. In Old Testament times, when a slave had served the same master for seven years, it was the master's duty to offer this slave freedom. But if the slave enjoyed working for this particular person, the slave could renounce his or her freedom, voluntarily saying, "I love my master. I do not wish to accept my freedom." Whereupon the master would take an awl and thrust it through the slave's earlobe, thus pinning the slave to the door. From that moment on everyone could see that such slaves had dedicated everything they had and everything they were for life to their masters.

As I meditated on this aspect of submission, my level of excitement rose. Submission, I saw, was nothing to do with spinelessness or imposed servility or even weakness. True submission demanded every ounce of strength and talent a person possessed. True submission was a voluntary donation of everything we have and everything we are to the loved one.

At that moment, I seemed to hear God say to me: "Don't you see that the stronger you are, and the more you grow and mature as a person, the more you have to give to David and your marriage?"

I did see. And at last I understood that everything that went into making me that "powerful woman" could be poured into our relationship to enrich and enhance it and to benefit David.

I turned to Proverbs 31 and saw how the powerful woman described there surrendered her many gifts—administration and counseling, tailoring and homemaking, to mention but a few—first to her husband, then to her family and then to the society in which she lived. I wanted to be submissive in that sense. Then and there, I asked God to release me from the condemnation I was under so that I could pour back into David's and my relationship everything that he had given me. The effect on my life and our marriage was startling. It was as though someone had smashed forever the mold into which I had been squeezed. I felt free—free from frustration, free to be the strong me God made me to be, free to give back to David the "powerful me" who existed chiefly because of the generosity of his love. Suddenly I felt fully alive. And because I was alive, our marriage came alive again as well.

Gone were the days when David was left to dream all the dreams for our marriage and execute all the plans. To abdicate responsibility for the relationship, I realized, was not submission but irresponsibility. We began to make plans together, pooled our ideas, donated to one another the differences of taste and spirituality and personality which we each bring to our relationship. As a result, our tired marriage sparkled again. David is still the head of this zestful relationship but now he has a cooperative helpmate and not a helpless one. Obeying the submission principle not only helped to mend our marriage, it goes on contributing to its sheer enjoyment.

Respect

Gill's marriage was saved when she recognized that she must surrender herself to her husband. My marriage was saved when I recognized that submission involved an effort—a positive donation of all I had and all I was to David. But submission has a third meaning: respect. Paul makes this clear when he says, "The wife must respect her husband" (Eph 5:33).

Selwyn Hughes tells the story of a woman whom God challenged through this verse. Her husband was not a Christian when she attended the marriage seminar where the life-transforming power of respect was underlined and where she was captivated with the thought that "God has given you the power to turn your man into the man both you and God want him to be—that power is power of respect."[31]

She resolved to develop within herself a deeper respect for her husband and watched him carefully while she prayed that God would alert her to praiseworthy parts of his personality and lifestyle. Gradually it dawned on her that her husband's disciplining of their children beautifully combined firmness and love. She also recognized just how trustworthy he was—he never broke a promise and he was scrupulously honest. Over the months she reflected back to him the worth she detected in him and showed him in a whole variety of ways how much she respected him.

Her husband, consequently, changed dramatically. He became more considerate and tolerant of her faith, for one thing, and even asked if he might accompany her to church. The day they went to church together, the minister preached one of the finest evangelistic sermons of his entire career, which resulted in the husband capitulating to the love of Jesus. Some time later he gave his testimony and this is what he said:

> When my wife began to show me respect, although I didn't realize what was happening, it created for me a bigger mold into which I wanted to pour myself. I wanted so much to be the man she saw me to be. And it was this that led eventually to my desire to receive Christ.[32]

The friend of mine who provided me with the diagram on how a couple can achieve both togetherness and "space" (chapter five), helped me to understand just why submission saves marriages. He drew a circle and divided it into six segments to represent those things psychologists tell us are necessary for our growth: love, acceptance, security, creativity, self-esteem and protection.

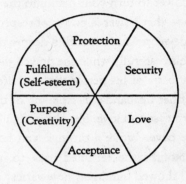

When a man lacks some of these resources, the circle of his life looks like this:

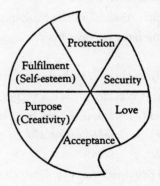

But when his wife submits, surrendering to him, donating her strengths to him and respecting him, she completes his circle and extends it. And the circle of his life expands to look like this:

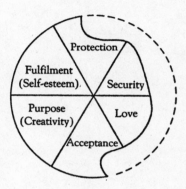

In other words, submitting brings healing. Even so, the challenge to submit is hard for the most committed wife. Her task is made ten times easier if her husband, too, will heed the instructions given in God's marriage manual, that is, love his wife as Christ loves the church.

CHAPTER 10

RESCUED BY LOVING LEADERSHIP

I ONCE ASKED MY HUSBAND, "WHY DID YOU MARRY ME?" HE paused, thought for a moment and then said, "In the past, when I took other girls out, I did it to make me happy. But when I met you, I knew I wanted to make you happy. That's why I married you."

This conversation flashed back into my mind as I began to prepare for this chapter because, as I have shown already in this book, our dreams of marriage did not materialize immediately. We had anticipated that, as soon as we were married, we would enjoy the depth of the companionship and intimacy God had in mind for couples when he created the marriage relationship. But this did not happen for us immediately. It took a minor marital breakdown to force us to take our car off the road, as it were, and to subject it to God's standards and the subsequent repairs before we began truly to understand and experience what this dimension of marriage entailed.

Like many of the couples I have introduced in this book, God stepped into our crisis in three main ways: with his own miracle-working touch, with wise counsel given through friends and by sending us back to his marriage manual, the Bible, with the mandate to obey the instructions we found there.

It was natural, therefore, that we should make a careful study of the Bible's teaching on headship. As I explained in chapter nine, in learning to submit I had been set free from the mold which had inhibited me for years. But we were conscious, of course, that headship and submission go together. It was not enough, therefore, to understand one without the other.

The discoveries we made as we meditated on this word *headship* changed our lives so dramatically that we always include teaching on the subject in our Marriage Fulfilment retreats, and it interests us to find that where husbands take this teaching seriously, marriages which seemed fit for the marital scrap-heap are being rescued, repaired and revitalized by God.

The Meaning of Headship

As we noted in the last chapter, the Bible leaves us in no doubt that just as the Father is the head of the Son and just as Jesus is the head of the church, so the husband is the head of the wife. Paul makes this clear in his letter to the Ephesians: "The husband is the head of the wife *as Christ is the head of the church*" (Eph 5:23, emphasis mine).

But we also noted in chapter nine that this headship has nothing to do with rights or privileges to be enjoyed. Rather it presupposes a willingness on the part of the male partner to shoulder certain heavy responsibilities. This becomes clear if we study Paul's teaching carefully. Contrary to traditional teaching, Paul nowhere gives the husband authority over his wife. Neither is he thinking of the controlling, directing function of the head when he uses this word to describe the husband's role in the marriage. As we have seen, when Paul wrote to the Ephesians, he knew nothing of neuroscience or the central nervous system. When he used the word *head* he thought, rather, of its integration with and nurture of the body rather than its control over the body. Paul makes this clear when he describes Christ as the head from whom the whole body is "joined and held together" and from which it "grows" (Eph 4:16).

Since Paul is not implying dictatorship with this title, headship, we need to tease out what he does mean. As David and I pondered over the implications of the word *head*, it became clear to us that Paul was trying to urge husbands to love their wives with the same superlative, unsurpassable standard of loving with which Jesus loves the church. We noticed, moreover, that Paul leaves husbands in no doubt about the nature of this dimension of loving.

He underlines that Jesus' love was a saving love. Jesus is the head of the church "of which he is the Savior" (Eph 5:23). This saving love involves a high degree of self-sacrifice: "Christ loved the church and gave himself up for her" (Eph 5:25). And Christ's motives were stunningly high. His plan is to make his bride holy, "to present her . . . without stain or wrinkle or any other blemish" (Eph 5:27). Since Jesus, the head of the church, loves the church like this, so the husband's headship demands that he will love his wife similarly.

Jesus' love, moreover, is a cherishing, caring, protective and nurturing love. The picture Paul uses to describe it is the manner with which a man treats his own body. As he so rightly points out, "no one ever hated his own body, but he feeds and cares for it, just as Christ does the church" (Eph 5:29). Since Jesus loves the church like that, the implication is that the husband's headship demands that he should love his wife likewise.

But, demanding though it is, this definition of headship is incomplete. In Paul's ode to love in 1 Corinthians 13 we read: "Love is patient, love is kind. It does not envy, it does not boast, it is not proud. It is not rude, it is not self-seeking, it is not easily angered, it keeps no record of wrongs. . . . It always protects, always trusts, always hopes, always perseveres" (1 Cor 13:4-7). Since these qualities are found in Jesus, the head of the church, they should be present in the husband also.

Yet even then the definition of headship remains incomplete, for if we are to take Jesus' pattern of headship seriously, we must notice that Jesus demonstrated not only a protecting, caring, cherishing, loving headship but also a gentle yet dynamic form of headship which is best summed up by the word *leadership*. Jesus' love was an authoritative (though not an authoritarian) love. And he gives us the reason why he could lead his bride, the church, with the kind of confidence and conviction which gave her such a sense of security. It was because he only passed on to the church the words he heard his Father speak and he only did the things his Father told him to do. In other words, he could afford to give guidance and impart wisdom because his was a praying, listening love. He was so in tune with the Father's will that the plans he made originated, not in his own mind or will, but with the Father. The husband who would exercise headship must learn, similarly, to become a praying, listening person.

Jesus' love was a sharing love. He allowed his disciples to witness the peaks of his joy, for example, on the Mount of Transfiguration. He also permitted them to witness the depths of his anguish, notably in Gethsemane. The implication is that the head of the home, the husband, by being similarly real with his wife, will encourage her to become real as well.

Supremely, Jesus' love is a forgiving, unbreakable love. That is why the symbol of Christianity is a cross, and that is also why the husband who would be head of the home must extend to his wife and family a sharing, caring, forgiving and unbreakable love.

Jesus himself took great trouble to demonstrate that his love is a serving love. So, on the night before he died, Jesus took a bowl and a towel and washed his disciples' dirty, sweaty feet, even though this was slaves' work. Moreover he made it clear to his disciples that he was setting them an example which he expected them to follow:

Do you understand what I have done for you? . . . You call me "Teacher" and "Lord," and rightly so, for that is what I am. Now that I, your Lord and Teacher, have washed your feet, you also should wash one another's feet. I have set you an example that you should do as I have done for you. . . . Now that you know these things, you will be blessed if you do them. . . . As I have loved you, so you must love one another. (Jn 13:12-15, 17, 34)

Just as husbands must follow this example of headship by performing menial tasks for their wives, so Jesus helps us to understand the true nature of headship when he says:

You know that the rulers of the Gentiles lord it over them, and their high officials exercise authority over them. Not so with you. Instead, whoever wants to become great among you must be your servant, and whoever wants to be first must be your slave—just as the Son of Man did not come to be served, but to serve, and to give his life as a ransom for many. (Mt 20:25-28)

As David Phypers sums up this question of headship:

Here is how I am to be the head of my wife: I am to love her with
the love of Jesus. Jesus' love does not demand love in return, but
gives and goes on giving even when that love is spurned. Jesus gave
up everything for the church—equality with God, heaven's glory,
eternal fellowship with the Father and the Holy Spirit, the right to
an earthly home, to a steady job, to the understanding and acclaim
of his fellows, to a fair trial and a humane death.[33]

An Improving, Unpossessive Love

As I typed out that definition of headship and the preceding list of
qualifications for headship, I realized that the demands laid on the
husband are awesome. No wonder our marriage suffered severe set-
backs. Such a high standard of loving is surely unattainable this side
of eternity. But, as God spurred David into action, he seemed to show
him the dimension of love I most needed at various stages of the healing
process of our marriage and encouraged him to work at one dimension
of loving at a time while I, meanwhile, worked at the discipline of
submission.

David had always tried to draw out my full potential. It was he who
encouraged me to write. It was he who encouraged me to take on
speaking engagements. It was he who encouraged me to train as a
counselor. And it was he who detected that I had a flair for leadership.
I saw none of these qualities in myself. He saw them and promoted
them. That is how the caterpillar of my former self became the butterfly it is today.

But a butterfly needs two things: a place to belong and freedom to
fly. One of the first challenges God required David to face was the need
to recognize that headship involved giving me both of these: roots and
wings.

To love me in this Christlike way was a struggle and a sacrifice for

David, I know. But just as Jesus commissioned his disciples to minister apart from him, so David set me free to develop my skills outside of the home and at a cost to himself. Consequently, our marriage was gradually enriched. I became a more interesting, alive, fulfilled person and had more to offer him, the entire family and our ministry together. And the paradox was that the more I tested my wings, the more I valued my roots and wanted David to know that my place of belonging—in him—was the most precious part of my life.

A Nurturing Love

David also took seriously the challenge of surrounding me with a nurturing love. He did this by finding a variety of ways of communicating the message: "I love you." For example, I have a passion for Mars candy bars. Whenever we travel abroad, I pine for them because either they are unobtainable in the country we're visiting or they are so expensive that pangs of guilt would plague me if I bought one.

On one of our trips abroad, when I opened my suitcase and started to unpack I found Mars bars in my shoes, Mars bars among my dresses and a layer of Mars bars lining the bottom of my suitcase. Before we had left home, David had smuggled one bar for every day of our trip into my packed bag.

Another time, on Mother's Day, I was feeling keenly the absence of our son who had recently moved for two years to a Third World country. David knew how said this Mother's Day could be for me, so he sent me a card which bore this message: "Happy Mother's Day. Glad you are the mother of our children. I love you very much. David." When a husband demonstrates his love in imaginative, creative, Christlike ways, the healing process is hastened.

I have a letter on my desk which convinces me that this loving leadership works, not just for us, but for others also. The letter is from a woman who had attended a meeting I had been addressing. Her husband was not a Christian. She had been a Christian for seven years at the time of writing. In her letter she expresses some of the feelings that rose to the surface in her while I was speaking:

I found the meeting very hard. . . . Soon after you started talking I started weeping and found it difficult to stop for much of the time. You seemed to be telling me a lot of things I didn't want to hear and yet I knew I must—all the ways I ought to be behaving in my situation, which sometimes seems soul-destroying. But through it all, many things came across to me in a whole new perspective as though I was hearing them clearly for the first time. At the end of it all I felt quite hopeless; that no matter how hard I tried I would not get the longed-for results. But somehow the Lord worked a miracle that afternoon, almost as though he knew how much I needed encouraging.

I had no sooner walked through the door than I was greeted with two lovely bunches of tulips from my eldest son who said it was his and Daddy's idea. I don't ever remember getting flowers like that before. This was swiftly followed by my husband offering to make me a cup of tea, again something that very rarely happens. By this time I was becoming somewhat bewildered! . . . But anyway, feeling tremendously encouraged I decided to try something that you had suggested and asked my husband to help me put the children to bed rather than stew quietly about the fact that he didn't—it worked! We had a lovely evening and the next morning he even joined us at church for our monthly family service. Praise the Lord! We had a lovely weekend.

A Serving Love
When David took seriously the example of the servanthood of Jesus

and began to express his love for me by performing menial tasks, my respect for him grew and my love for him deepened.

I recall a day when snow was falling relentlessly onto the road outside our house. When I looked out of my study window onto the street below, I could see only one solitary figure. I wondered who would venture out in such conditions. A few minutes later, my husband came into the house looking like a snowman. Snow had settled on his graying hair and his navy overcoat, and his face was blue with cold. When I asked him what he had been doing he simply said, "I've been trying to thaw the locks of the car so that you can keep your hospital appointment this afternoon."

I was humbled. And I realized that this was what Jesus meant by headship; that when a husband expresses his headship through sacrificial love, it is easy to submit to him in the same way as we submit to Jesus.

Just as this kind of self-giving leadership helped to save our marriage, so this Christlike approach to headship contributed to the mending of a marriage I mentioned in an earlier chapter: the Gary-Karen partnership. As I explained, when Gary was pastoring a church, his wife Karen committed adultery and intended to leave him. But when God mended their marriage Gary's whole attitude changed. As Karen compares the past with the present:

It is not unusual to drive by our home and see Gary outside hanging clothes on the line. He has changed drastically in what he does in our home. When our children were young, he never once got up with them in the night; he felt it was my responsibility. Now he willingly gets up to give a drink or medicine to a needy child. . . . Gary also regularly helps me with the dishes and many times does them alone if I'm involved with something else. He is now the one who gets up and makes breakfast for the children.[34]

A Healing Love

Gary also expressed his headship by helping to heal Karen's wounds, even though she had received those wounds as a result of her unfaithfulness to him. This was a wonderful gift to Karen. As Karen describes the wonder of it all:

> Guilt was one of my biggest enemies. . . . Gary had forgiven me from his heart, and I knew the Lord had forgiven me. Yet it was hard to *feel* forgiven. I felt like I had a scarlet A glowing from my chest. I knew that I was like everyone else—a sinner—but I felt so much worse. . . . At times I experienced sudden surges of guilt. While sitting in church, I would feel like everyone was looking at me. "She committed adultery; she was with another man." These thoughts taunted me till I wanted to run and escape the looks I imagined other people were giving me. One Sunday I started crying and quickly went to an adjacent room before anyone saw me. Gary followed me. I turned to him and cried, "Gary, I just can't take it! I know what people are thinking."
>
> Gary held me close. . . . We prayed. . . . After some time I was able to regain enough composure to go back to the service.[35]

In his poem "A Healing Season," Gary reflects on the mixture of feelings which flooded his heart as he watched God's love touch his wife through his loving leadership and wash away the hurts of the past:

> *A Healing Season*
> She cried tonight.
> Tears of remorse and concern
> flowed from her soul
> for our destruction.
>
> She sighed softly.
> Quietly resigning herself

to the rebuilding
of our love.

She smiled today.
Not very deep or extended,
yet betraying healing
deep within her soul.

She laughed aloud.
An honest, hearty sound,
responding in true joy
to a renewed me.

We touched at last.
Each reaching deeply
to grasp the self
of the other.[36]

An Authoritative Love

This challenge to loving leadership helped Dave and Gill, whom I
mentioned in the last chapter, to experience God's healing of their
relationship. Shortly after his baptism, Dave came across Paul's injunc-
tion: "Husbands, love your wives, just as Christ loves the church"
(Eph 5:25). He recognized that his responsibility was to take this exhortation as seriously as Gill was responding to the challenge to submit.
He could see that God was changing Gill, causing the fruit of the Spirit
to mature in her, especially with patience, peace and gentleness, and
that this was making her more easy to live with. Now it was his turn
to ask God to change him—to teach him how to love his wife.

Jesus' love is an authoritative love, as we have seen. He knows how to hear the Father's voice. He is determined to obey his Father's will at all costs. He never passes on to his bride plans which promote himself or his own best interests. Instead, he waits to discern the Father's plans and only passes on to her the proposals that originate in the mind of God. As Dave reflected on these facts, this is what he said: What a challenge. I don't even know how to be assertive—but when Gill's got crises and comes to me I need to know how to be assertive and calm her down. I'm working on that. And I'm learning to listen to God, too, and to really wait until I've got answers. I've never prayed like that before.

When Dave made this admission, I could tell that Gill was proud of him and respected him for every sign of spiritual growth and personal maturity. She felt cherished just by the assurance that Dave was asking God to work deeply in his life.

Cherishing love was another aspect of the love Jesus demonstrated which had impressed itself on Dave. He told me how he was trying to imitate the heavenly Bridegroom: "I'm trying to read Gill's nonverbal signs. I need to be sensitive to know how to deal with situations when they arise. There are lots of signs that you just have to pick up without her telling you."

Gill observed that, as far as she was concerned, this cherishing was the most cementing quality about their newly-styled relationship. It affected every part of their marriage, including the sexual side which had posed so many problems previously. As Dave put it: "I've not got a lot of experience as far as sex is concerned, and I have to learn as fast as I can what makes Gill happy. I'm working hard on that too." And, in doing this homework faithfully, Dave and Gill are discovering the truth of John Powell's claim that love works for those who work at it. They are also discovering that, when a husband loves his wife as Jesus calls him to—giving her the loving, sensitive leadership she craves and which fills her with a sense of well-being—even the most battered marriage can be mended quite fast.

Cherishing Love: Len and Linda's Story

The challenge to love as Jesus loved—to cherish one's wife—came to Len when his marriage to Linda was in crisis.

Len and Linda had not been married long when they suffered the trauma of the death of their first baby. As Linda explained to me:

Losing the baby seemed to destroy what little we had in terms of a marriage which was not really very well founded at that stage because we had not been married for very long. I think my first reaction to the whole thing was to be very, very angry and that anger seemed at first to convey itself to Len. I wanted to blame Len. It was easy to say I wasn't given the right support when I was pregnant. Our marriage was not strong enough to hold it together. The loss of the baby exposed the lack of reality in our marriage. We were living on the romantic past—that's all we really knew of one another. But losing the baby seemed to break down everything we had. I'd been a Christian for about ten years but it was as if everything I'd ever believed in my Christian life had suddenly been thrown away—as if I didn't even know God and knew very little about him. My resentment was so great I couldn't stretch out and feel God's touch.

And Len recalled the confusion the loss of the baby plunged him into:

I wanted to run away from the whole affair just to get it behind me and forget it—but I had the responsibility of a husband. So I had to stand up and support not only myself but also Lin in her emotional state. I found that very difficult. I found my own emotions were unfathomable—pretty hard to explain at the time. I couldn't say I had any feelings. It was almost like there was a void. My subconscious was suppressing the hurts and resentments and angers that may have been there. But people were telling me: "You've got to support Lin in this. You've got to stand by her." It was very difficult. Up to that point I had felt an onlooker so far as the baby was concerned. I was just pushed aside only to be drawn upon when there was a need. All I wanted to do was to run away but this bond of marriage was holding me there. The whole of my past life was to run away from situations that were difficult and not to face up to them. So on the one hand I had that pulling me one way and on the other hand the marriage was saying, "No, you've got to stay. You've got to experience this."

Len did stay. And, as best he could, he gave Lin the cherishing love she craved. It was far from easy because the foundations of the marriage had never been laid. But God moved in and equipped them with the firmest foundations any marriage can have: the instructions to marrieds we find in his Word. Now, five years further on, they have this to say:

We're a lot closer together now. We share a lot more. We talk a lot more. And we care a lot more for each other. We tend to recognize each other's needs and act upon them, whereas when we were first married we were selfish.

A Sharing, Caring Love

Len admitted to me that God challenged him not simply to cherish Lin while she was vulnerable but also to share his own vulnerability with her. This went right against the grain for him:

Suddenly being thrown into a situation where we had to be real with each other, we were very defensive. We wanted to keep our grief to ourselves and not show our real feelings to each other. For myself, as a man and from a large family of six brothers and one sister, to have to show my feelings through grief seemed like an act of weakness. But we had to let those barriers down and be vulnerable, real. It was very painful but God came into the pain and healed it. As Len dared to be vulnerable with Lin, so she expressed her grief to him. She admits that this was not something she was used to doing. She was the independent type, self-contained. But she learned, through the death of her baby, that when she allows Len to glimpse her inner-most feelings she gives to him the privilege of loving her as Jesus loves the church. She also opens the door to the kind of communication which makes couples real to one another.

"The Years the Locusts Have Eaten"

I once saw a program on television which reminded me of Gary and Karen, and Dave and Gill, and Len and Lin, and several of the other couples I have mentioned in this book.

A farmer in South Africa stood beside his crop of corn which had grown to a healthy height of seven feet and was ripening fast. This farmer then turned over in his hands all that was left of his harvest: a series of stalks stripped of their leaves and measuring less than one foot. He explained that a swarm of locusts had descended on his land and within half an hour had eaten every inch of goodness. He was left with nothing but stubble.

The fields of stubble seemed to represent the marriages ravaged by crises. But as the cameras zoomed in on the giant locusts, a promise God gave through the prophet Joel rang through my mind: "I will give you back what you lost in the years when swarms of locusts ate your crops. . . . You will praise the LORD your God, who has done won-derful things for you" (Joel 2:25-26 TEV).

As I put together the pictures and the promise, I marveled. We whose marriages were once like that scene of dereliction know that the impossible is possible; that God can restore the years the locusts have eaten. He has proved it by mending our marriages.

EPILOG

THE BEST IS YET TO BE

THIS BOOK WAS FINISHED. I HAD RETURNED HOME FROM THE COTtage where I had retreated to write. The completed manuscript was in its brown envelope ready to be sent to the publisher. But before I had had time to mail it, a letter arrived which prompted me to add this postscript. The letter was from a woman I had never met. She poured out her story of a marriage which had started disastrously, which had gone from bad to worse and which seemed now to be teetering on the brink of total collapse. But she concluded her letter with a question which pierced my heart: "Is there *any* way our relationship can still be renewed?"

While I was wondering how best to respond to my correspondent's cry for help, my husband and I led a Marriage Fulfilment retreat many miles from our home. Several couples in key positions of Christian leadership attended this particular retreat, and many of them confided in us that their marriages had received severe and serious blows over the years. Some couples, it seemed, had broken almost every rule in God's book, yet they were clinging on to the remnants of their once-loving relationships.

As I listened to these sad stories, tears would sometimes stream down my face as I would be reminded afresh how two people who have been in love can so wound one another. There were times when anger would burn in my heart, as I heard and saw for myself how subtle and effective Satan's assaults on Christian marriages still are. The fight against the enemy does not diminish with the years, but rather seems to grow fiercer. At times I thought my heart would break as I watched two desperate people— husband and wife—lay before me the pieces of the jigsaw of their past and ask whether these pieces could ever create a whole and beautiful picture again.

Each couple seemed to echo the desperate question I'd received in the mail: "Is it possible, even at this eleventh hour, for our marriage to be saved?"

As my husband and I attempted to respond to that question, I thought of this book and realized that some of its readers might similarly be looking for a succinct, yet insightful and sensitive, answer to that question. And so, in this postscript, I have tried to summarize further some of the secrets which have helped us and which we delight in sharing with hurting couples.

I pray that many of my readers will take seriously the suggestions outlined here, that they will find these suggestions to be tools which will make the rebuilding of their marriages not only possible but pleasurable and that the result will be a dimension of marital love which exceeds their wildest dreams and hopes.

Daring to Believe in Miracles

The first step is to *believe that the age of miracles is not yet past*. I say that because when life is tough, and our relationships with our partners feel more painful than joyful, it sometimes seems as though we shall go mad with the hopelessness of it all. At such times it often feels as though God has deserted us, as though our prayers are like boomerangs which rise toward heaven but then return to earth again, failing utterly to reach the ears of God.

At times like these we are in desperate need of objectivity. And the objective truth is that the God whom we worship is a supernatural God. It is God who controls the seasons, who determines the number of stars and names them, who orchestrates the heavens with its billions of galaxies and harmonizes it with the earth which he has filled with a whole variety of flora and fauna. It is God who energizes the universe and sustains it. It is God who designed the vastness of space—that expanse of his creation which would take 80,000 light years to traverse (a light year is almost six million million miles).

This God who is so great that he defies comprehension is the same God who holds our marriages in the palm of his hand. This God has promised to involve himself in our lives: "I know the plans I have for you . . . plans to prosper you and not to harm you, plans to give you hope and a future" (Jer 29:11). This God delights to perform miracles for married people as the couples mentioned in this book delight to testify.

But, of course, we must never fall into the trap of believing God to be the heavenly magician who sits in the heavenly places waving a wand over our lives to right all the wrongs. No, we are adults and God expects adults to cooperate with him when he unleashes his miracle-working, creative energy into our lives and relationships. So the second step we must take is to *recommit ourselves to our relationship*. Sometimes, at the end of a Marriage Fulfilment retreat, we invite couples to reaffirm their marriage vows in a simple service which forms the climax of the conference. This is always a most moving occasion. Sometimes couples have to struggle to reach this place of renewed commitment. As one woman who for several months had been tempted to walk out on her husband explained to me:

> My commitment to make our marriage work had been nonexistent. When it came, it grew and grew—and that can only have been through the intervention of the Holy Spirit. I decided that I *would* work at our relationship; that we would not only get through this sticky patch but that we would emerge and we would be stronger. I knew, despite the many hurts my husband had inflicted on me, that I was totally committed to keep us together. Since making that commitment, I know that a miracle has happened. We have moved from bitter distance to happy companionship. God's power is enormous. The best is yet to be.

If we ask God, the author of marriage, to intervene on our behalf and if we will cooperate, he will surprise us with joy and pour into our hearts the strength and the resolve to take the third step, which is to *let our partner off the hook*.

When our relationship lies in ruins on the shore of our lives, it is almost certain that our partner has failed us abysmally over the years. We may well be conscious that it is not simply our marriage that is in a mess. We, ourselves, may also feel we are a wreck. We may be riddled with feelings of insecurity, be unable to see any worth in ourselves, feel compelled to wear masks so that the people around us are prevented from discerning what we are really like.

It is important, if we are serious about seeking God's healing for our relationships, that we recognize the truth of the situation. We must stop pretending. We must feel afresh the full brunt of the pain our partners have inflicted on us. This will be neither easy nor pleasant. But having acknowledged these facts we are then in a position to let our partners off the hook; to resolve not to harbor the memory of past hurts any longer nor to keep a score of past wrongs but rather, with an act of the will, to forgive our offending, imperfect partners for the damage done; to begin to love again. This can be a most liberating moment, as I have explained in the chapter on forgiveness. It can be the beginning of a whole new era of our marriages.

I remember the time when God brought me to this place of healing prayer. I had been pouring into his lap the resentment and bitterness I at that time felt against my husband. Gradually the Holy Spirit convicted me that anger, resentment, bitterness and stored-up wraths from the past are sins to be confessed, not trophies to be prized. It was as though the sword of God had pierced my soul to wound me. But it was not the wound that would slay; rather, it was more like the wound of the surgeon's scalpel, the wound which heals. For the first time in years, I acknowledged that I was as much at fault as my husband. Humbled and contrite, penitent and deeply sorrowful, I knelt, as it were, at the foot of Christ's cross and confessed the many ways in which I myself had failed our marriage and therefore had failed my husband.

God had been teaching me that confession without repentance (the determination to live differently) is incomplete and that confession and repentance must be capped by receiving his free gift of forgiveness. And so, with gratitude, I received from God the cleansing I needed which seemed to dislodge the silt of years. A gradual change crept over me. My attitude to my husband changed. The hardness toward him melted.

So our marriage changed, even though the circumstances surrounding it and exerting pressure on it did not change. Such is the power of God's grace.

God Heals the Brokenhearted

One of my favorite hymns makes this claim:

> I cannot tell how silently He suffered,
> As with His peace He graced this place of tears,
> Or how His heart upon the cross was broken,
> The crown of pain to three and thirty years,
> But this I know, He heals the brokenhearted,
> And stays our sin, and calms our lurking fear,
> And lifts the burden from the heavy laden,
> For yet the Savior, Savior of the world, is here.

The reason why I love that hymn is that the more involved I become in helping people unravel the tangled threads of an unhappy marriage, the more convinced I become that the hurts which one or both partners bring to the relationship make a major contribution toward the disintegration of the marriage, unless healing of those hurts happens. These hurts often make serious though invisible and often indefinable inroads into the relationship, forcing the marriage onto a collision course. Let me use a personal illustration to explain what I mean.

When my husband and I married, our expectations of one another were high. We both longed for the intimacy which marriage seemed to offer and we believed that our deepest, innermost needs could be met in one another. What we did not realize as, with the utmost sincerity, we promised to love one another "for better, for worse, for richer, for poorer" was that our lives are rather like the proverbial iceberg. What appears above the surface is a mere fraction of the whole. And what I certainly did not anticipate was that certain fears which lurked below the surface in me would prevent us from enjoying the closeness we both craved.

Part of the problem was that, over the years, I found it more and more difficult to believe David when he told me how much he loved me. I saw how this fear distressed my husband. I condemned myself for being so faithless. I confessed this personal failure, believing it to be a sin. But nothing changed. We were no nearer finding a solution to the problem than we had been when we first married.

One day, as though in answer to my prayer that God would bring some new insight into this seemingly hopeless situation, I vividly recalled, play by play, an incident which had happened when I was a child of five or six. I had been extremely naughty. In my mind's eye, I recalled how hard my father had spanked me. I ran to my bedroom for refuge but my father followed me, forced me to come downstairs and told me, in front of my mother and brothers, that I had been so naughty that they did not want me anymore. His face was flushed with anger; and he wagged a fat finger in my frightened face as he told me to go back to my room, pack my belongings in a bag and leave home.

As I continued to relive this painful piece of personal history, it was as though I became the forlorn little girl in the pictures being flashed on the screen of my mind. I felt the panic rise as I pushed my few belongings into a bag. And I felt the pain in the palm of my hand as my father pressed into it the sixpenny piece which was to pay my bus fare to the Dr. Barnardo's home where he said I was to live from now on.

My mother was crying as I stumbled out of the house. Numb with fright and feeling very alone, I walked down the street of terraced houses where we lived and had almost reached the bus stop at the end of the road when I heard footsteps behind me. It was my mother running and calling my pet name: "Joycie! Joycie!" She grabbed me by the hand and tried to pull me back home. But I protested, frightened that if I returned my father might hit me again—or worse still, refuse to have me back.

I was attending a meeting when this memory rose to the surface of my mind. The series of pictures I was watching was so vivid that I was scarcely aware that I was crying quietly but persistently. Two people came to me and asked me what the problem was. When I explained the situation to them, they laid hands on me and prayed a brief, though authoritative, prayer in which they asked God to break the power that memory had over me so that it would lose forever its power to affect my behavior as an adult.

The first thing I noticed after this meeting was that instead of looking for rejection around every corner (and, like others who search for it, finding rejection around every corner), I began to take risks in relationships which I would not have taken previously. To my surprise, these risks resulted not in rejection but in acceptance and deepened friendships.

But it was not until my birthday ten months later that I realized just how effective this prayer had been. Because my father's severe discipline had taught me to fear that people who say they love me would one day reject me, I had always secretly dreaded my birthday. What if a significant person, perhaps my husband, forgot that it was my birthday? Wouldn't that prove that the person didn't really want me but only tolerated my existence?

On my forty-ninth birthday, I was sitting at my desk working when some words from Psalm 139 began to run through my mind: "You knit me together in my mother's womb. . . . I praise you because I am fearfully and wonderfully made" (Ps 139:13-14). These words were familiar and well-loved. Yet the reminder of them caused me to leap

to my feet and lean, dazed, against the window where I gazed at my
neighbor's garden and tried to drink in the truth of what was happening
to me. For the first time in my life, I could pray the words of this psalm
with integrity. For the first time in my life, I could thank God for the
gift of life. For the first time in my life, I could thank him that I had
been born.

When I went back to my desk, I grew excited because suddenly I saw
clearly what had happened all those years ago. With the wisdom of
hindsight and the perception of adulthood, it now became crystal clear
that my parents had tried to teach me a salutary lesson: that unaccep-
table behavior must be punished. They had never intended to scar my
sensitive spirit. It had never occurred to them that their small daughter
would absorb that crippling message: "You're not wanted, only tolerated." I could therefore leave behind forever this legacy from my past
and believe that when people, and particularly my husband, say they
love me they mean it.

I spent some time thinking through what had happened to me over
the years. Of course, I had not realized that this childhood incident had
affected me so deeply. I had forgotten it—or so I thought. I had no idea
that it had given birth to a fear which had taken root in my self-
conscious. Indeed, this fear lurked, unacknowledged and unrecognized
for much of my life, until I married. But it had become a part of my
make-up.

Because the husband-wife relationship involves the same closeness
and intimacy of the parent-child relationship, and because trust is vital
to a marriage, the consequences of this childhood experience had sur-
faced shortly after my marriage and had played havoc with my relationship with David ever since. As I recall the pain and the consequent
healing, I rejoice in the sheer goodness and generosity of God in ridding
me of this obstacle which hindered my growth for so long.

Trusting God to Show the Way

Countless couples are in need of such healing. Francis MacNutt, in his excellent book *Healing*, reminds us that this kind of healing is often called for in certain circumstances: whenever people become aware that they are held down in any way by ancient hurts or memories; whenever any unreasonable or irrational fear or anxiety or compulsion prevents them from behaving in a normal, loving, Christlike manner; or whenever the freedom they should be enjoying in Christ is obstructed in some way.

The root of this pain may find its origins in the dim and distant past, as in my own experience. On the other hand, the bondage may boast a more recent origin: the death of a child, the loss of some status or fond friend, a change of lifestyle which leaves us disorientated, a particular disappointment. We need, therefore, to seek from God the necessary discernment to determine the length of the taproot and the method he has chosen to deal with it.

The way God moves in to touch these open wounds and to heal them so that they lose their power to paralyze us is unique to each person. It is as varied as the expressions of God's creativity in nature. On the occasion I have highlighted, the time available for prayer was short and God worked swiftly by simply breaking the power of the memory. On other occasions it is enough to pray that the sting of the memory will be removed. But often the prayer for healing will take a different turn.

The person in pain needs to be invited to describe the area of hurt in detail; to expose the repressed memories and feelings to the light of consciousness; to remember the painful event from the past as vividly as possible. The people praying for this person will then seek, in one way or another, to bring the power of the risen Lord to the hidden hurts so that these are healed and transformed. Alternatively, they may pray that the salve of the Holy Spirit may be applied to the specific

sores which have been exposed. It is always advisable to ask God to
fill with his love all the places which have lain empty and loveless over
the years.

Roger Hurding explains the nature of this healing:

Our past is an open book to God, a book in which the pages can
be turned back with a sense of Christ's companionship, revealing
those blotted paragraphs we had forgotten about, the pictures of
which we are ashamed, the leaves that have stuck together through
life's spillages. . . . The book can be restored, its whole story know
the refreshment of the Spirit and so become clearer, a less com-
promised tale to be told to the glory of its divine author.[37]

Because God delights to restore the soiled and scarred manuscript
of our lives, the fifth step couples may need to take is *to seek from God
the necessary healing.* But, of course, having received our healing we
must take the sixth step: to live within that healing, facing up to its
implications. Sometimes, I realize, this is easier said than done.

One of the chief purposes of this book has been to help couples to
discover how best they can work the ingredients of God's recipe for
marriage into their relationships. But even when we know the theory,
translating it into practice is often far from easy. For this reason, many
of us need help from others so that we do resolve to break old habits
and adopt new thought patterns and lifestyles. The seventh step is to
*meet regularly with another couple who is as motivated about remaking their
marriage as you are.*

My husband and I have proved the value of this. At one stage of the
marriage-mending process for us, we would meet monthly with a couple we trusted, enjoy a relaxed meal together and then discuss one
aspect of Christian marriage which concerned both couples at that
particular time. Each couple would express why they found it difficult
to put this particular portion of the Bible's teaching into practice. Each

couple would seek to encourage the other to find constructive ways of bringing their marriage into alignment with God's teaching. And each couple would help the other to discover where their expectations were realistic and where expectations might need to be pruned or changed.

I recommend this practice. If you know of a suitable couple who could support you in this way, I suggest that you take this seventh step and perhaps use the questions in the appendix of this book to explore possible ways forward for you and your partner. You then will have the support you need to tackle step eight: *to stand against the enemy whose mission in life is to destroy Christian marriages.*

The Need to Resist the Evil One
The battle is on. Evil is both a reality within us and around us. Paul reminds us of the nature of the opposition:

> For we are not fighting against people made of flesh and blood, but against persons without bodies—the evil rulers of the unseen world, those mighty satanic beings and great evil princes of darkness who rule this world; and against huge numbers of wicked spirits in the spirit world. (Eph 6:12 LB)

Paul goes on to instruct us what to do: "Resist the enemy whenever he attacks" (Eph 6:13 LB).

This applies in particular to couples who become conscious that their relationship seems to be in the direct firing line of Satan's shells and bullets. Together with our partner we must resist Satan. We must avoid falling into the trap of begging God to do it all. We ourselves have the authority to stand on the name of Jesus and to command the enemy to go; to counter every Satanic attack with active resistance. And the enemy has no alternative but to slink away—at least for a while.

Because the battle often rages with frightening ferocity and because we frequently feel so frail, the ninth step is this: *ask others to pray for you*. We need never be ashamed of admitting that we cannot survive without the prayer support of others. And we need never fear that such prayer is second rate or of little worth. God seemed to remind me of that fact while I was working on the closing paragraphs of this book. I was trying to help a couple in distress and was conscious that, for much of the time, I could do little but pray for them. On a day when feelings of helplessness almost overwhelmed me, a letter arrived from someone I have never met. He enclosed a text which bore the following encouragement:

> *The Power of Prayer*
> The day was long, the burden I had borne
> Seemed heavier than I could longer bear,
> And then it lifted—but I did not know
> Some one had knelt in prayer;
> Had taken me to God that very hour,
> And asked the easing of the load, and He,
> In infinite compassion, had stooped down
> And taken it from me.
>
> We cannot tell how often as we pray
> For some bewildered one, hurt and distressed,
> The answer comes, but many times those hearts
> Find sudden peace and rest.
>
> Some one had prayed, and Faith, a reaching hand,
> Took hold of God, and brought Him down that day!
> So many, many hearts have need of prayer:
> Oh, let us pray!

Let us ask others to pray and, when necessary, take the tenth and most costly step of all: *to ask others to help us* find our way through our valley of weeping and to stay alongside us in the pain and frustration until this valley becomes, for us, the place of laughter and joy which the psalmist describes in Psalm 84.

Paul exhorts us to bear one another's burdens. And there are times when we need more than prayer—we need care and the counsel of others. To seek such help is not a sign of weakness. It is a sign of strength because it takes courage to make such a request.

My husband and I will be indebted forever to those who stayed alongside us while God tested the metal from which our relationship was made. Without their help and support, our marriage would have collapsed. With it, the metal increased in strength.

More and more churches are taking seriously their responsibility to provide a team of people equipped to come alongside those who seek such help. It is my personal prayer that soon we shall see a nationwide network of such Christians who are competent to help couples who send out distress signals. I pray God will raise up people who will incarnate God's love to couples in crisis, people who will give generously of their time and themselves that they may witness the miracle which prompted the writing of this book: a whole series of marriages on the mend.

Questions to Discuss

Chapter 1: Though God sometimes mends marriages suddenly, he may choose a method with us that requires hard work on our part. Why would it be worth it to you?

Chapter 2: How do I feel you could best demonstrate to me that, after God, I am number one in your life?

Chapter 3: How can we guarantee that we spend quality time together each day? each week?

Chapter 4: How do I feel we could improve the quality of our communication?

Chapter 5: How do I feel about our social oneness? How do I feel we could improve it?

How do I feel when you want to do things on your own—apart from me?

How do I feel about the amount of space and togetherness there is in our relationship at the moment?

How do I feel about the way we cope with crises?

Chapter 6: How do I feel about our prayer times together and apart?

Chapter 7: How do I feel about our sex life?

Chapter 8: Is there something in our relationship I need to forgive? something I need to ask forgiveness about?

Chapter 9: How do I feel about donating all I have and am to you?

Chapter 10: How do I feel about drawing out your potential as a person?

How do I feel about committing myself to our relationship for the rest of my life?

Notes

Preface
[1]*Care Trust News*, No. 8, April/May 1985, p. 30.

Chapter 1
[2]Joyce Huggett, *Two into One* (Downers Grove, Ill.: InterVarsity Press, 1981), p. 126.
[3]Joyce Huggett, *We Believe in Marriage* (London: Marshalls, 1982), p. 55.
[4]Gwen Wilkerson, *In His Strength* (Ventura, Calif.: Regal Books, 1978), p. 38.
[5]Ibid., p. 95.
[6]Ibid., p. 96.
[7]Ibid., p. 98.

Chapter 2
[8]"The Marriage Service," *Alternative Service Book* (Oxford: Oxford University Press, 1980), p. 293.
[9]Antoine de Saint-Exupery, *The Little Prince* (London: Piccolo, 1974), pp. 66-67.

Chapter 3
[10]David Atkinson, *To Have and To Hold* (London: Collins, 1979), chapter 3.
[11]Eileen Vincent, *God Can Do It Here* (London: Marshalls, 1982), chapter 23.
[12]David Watson, in a tape entitled *The Suffering Servant* (Eastbourne: ICC Studios, 1983).

Chapter 4
[13]Wilkerson, *In His Strength*, p. 99.
[14]John Powell, *The Secret of Staying in Love* (Harlow: Argus, 1974), p. 78.
[15]John Powell, *Will The Real Me Please Stand Up* (Harlow: Argus, 1985), p. 9.
[16]Ibid., p. 14.
[17]Ibid., p. 16.

Chapter 5
[18]Sheldon Vanauken, *A Severe Mercy* (London: Hodder and Stoughton, 1977), p. 35.
[19]Joyce Huggett, *Two into One*, p. 12.

Chapter 6
[20]Andy Butcher, "Conversion," *Family Magazine*, March 1986.

Chapter 7
[21]Karen Kuhne, *A Healing Season* (London: Marshalls, 1984), p. 76.
[22]Ibid., p. 79.
[23]Ibid., pp. 126-27.
[24]Ibid., p. 140.
[25]Ibid., p. 150.
[26]Ibid., p. 150.

Chapter 8
[27]Neville Ward, *Friday Afternoon* (London: Epworth, 1976) p. 26.
[28]Ibid., p. 19.
[29]Powell, *The Secret of Staying in Love*, p. 147.

Chapter 9
[30]Powell, *The Secret of Staying in Love*, p. 146.
[31]Selwyn Hughes, *Marriage as God Intended* (Eastbourne: Kingsway, 1983), p. 39.
[32]Ibid., p. 40.

Chapter 10
[33]David Phypers, *Christian Marriage in Crisis* (Bromley: Marc Europe, 1985), p. 23.
[34]Kuhne, *A Healing Season*, p. 146.
[35]Ibid., pp. 141-42.
[36]Ibid., p. 151.

Epilogue
[37]Roger Hurding, *Roots and Shoots* (London: Hodder and Stoughton, 1986), p. 366.